THE
Anniversary
Compulsion

THE
Anniversary Compulsion

CANADA'S CENTENNIAL CELEBRATIONS
A MODEL MEGA-ANNIVERSARY

PETER H. AYKROYD

Dundurn Press
Toronto and Oxford
1992

EDITOR: Kathryn J. Dean
COPY EDITOR: June Trusty
DESIGN AND TYPESETTING: ArtPlus Limited/Brant Cowie
PRINTING AND BINDING: John Deyell Company

The publisher wishes to acknowledge the generous assistance and ongoing support of **The Canada Council**, **The Book Publishing Industry Development Programme** of the **Department of Communications**, **The Ontario Publishing Centre** of the **Ministry of Culture and Communications** and **The Ontario Arts Council.**

Care has been taken to trace the ownership of copyright material used in the text, including the illustrations. The author and publisher welcome any information enabling them to rectify any reference or credit in subsequent editions.

J. Kirk Howard, Publisher

Canadian Cataloguing in Publication Data

Aykroyd, Peter H.

The anniversary compulsion: Canada's centennial celebrations (sub-1), a model mega-anniversary

Includes bibliographical references and index.
ISBN 1-55002-185-0

1. Canada – Centennial celebrations, etc.
I. Title

FC623.C4A93 1992   394.2'68471   C92-095335-2
F1034.3.A93   1992

Dundurn Press Limited
2181 Queen Street East
Suite 301
Toronto, Canada
M4E 1E5

Dundurn Distribution
73 Lime Walk
Headington
Oxford, England
OX3 7AD

Contents

To the women and men at every level who comprised the staff of the Centennial Commission, 1963–67. Members of a team. Without them, the Centennial could not have happened. All deserve an accolade, and it is regrettable that in this book it was possible to mention only a few of them by name.

Acknowledgements

IN THE PREPARATION OF THIS WORK I am indebted to many people. In no particular order:

To Dr. Gerald O. Barney, executive director of the Institute for 21st Century Studies, Arlington, Virginia, for urging me to write.

To Lorraine Helene Gougeon, my wife, who suffered my remoteness while I toiled on the text at our residences in Kingston, Ontario, and Coronado, California.

To Kathryn Dean, who turned the first and second drafts inside out and upside down, and helped me transform a heap of pages into a book. A brilliant editor.

To June Trusty, who as copy/production editor brought additional polish to the final work.

To Dr. Donald Swainson, an acknowledged scholar of the Confederation period, professor in the History Department at Queen's University, Kingston, who read the confederation history chapter and kindly gave me a passing grade.

To the indefatigable John W. Irwin, who found me a publisher and shepherded the book through the publication process.

To my great friend Miller Alloway, who has forgotten more about publishing and printing than I will ever know.

To Brenda Smith, Lisa Pastrana and Terry-Lee Haase, who faithfully and accurately helped to input the one hundred thousand words.

To Carolyn Quinn, who with Jungian synchronicity appeared at my elbow like an angel, in the bowels of the National Archives, seeking on the same day, and the same hour, the very Centennial material that I had just called up. We were the only two people in twenty-four years to do so. She became my contract researcher, finding things for me that I did not have the wit to uncover.

To Mary-Ann Simpkins, who hunted down the photos and the credits.

To His Honour Judge Marcel Joyal, sometime executive assistant to Maurice Lamontagne, who helped me appreciate the value of this unassuming man.

To my accomplished sister Judith Harvie and her very literate husband Eric, who kindly read the final draft and lovingly showed me how to make it better.

To Robbins Elliott, who refreshed my memory on certain details, and a person who could have written a much more comprehensive book and has to suffer the lacunae and weaknesses that I am sure are present, all of which must be attributed to me, and me alone.

Peter H. Aykroyd
Kingston, Ontario
August 1992

Preface

It's December 31, 1966. Nighttime. A few hours to go before midnight. The scene is Parliament Hill in Ottawa. The seat of the Government of Canada. A foot of snow covers the broad sweep in front of the Parliament Buildings. The sky is overcast and a steady north wind whistles in over the white-coated Gatineau Hills. The Pre-Cambrian Shield. Oldest exposed rocks in the world. On the weather map in *U.S.A. Today,* this part of North America would show up purple from November to April. This is *North.*

Nothing unusual so far. But wait. What is this? On the snowy field, bleachers have been erected. The Royal Canadian Mounted Police band is playing. And there in the dark and biting cold sits The Right Honourable Lester Bowles Pearson, ninth prime minister of Canada, in a black cashmere overcoat, black Homburg hat, red wool scarf and fur-lined black leather gloves. He is smiling. Beside him sits The Honourable Julia Verlyn "Judy" LaMarsh, his secretary of state, swaddled in black mink with a matching black mink hat, fur-lined snow-boots, fur-lined gloves. She is also smiling.

Surrounding them sit a couple hundred people clad in similar garb. This is not a night to *sit* out in the cold. What are they doing out here in the middle of the night looking pleased? Are they pretending, or is this for real?

What they are doing has never happened before and probably will never happen again. They are here to usher in Canada's Centennial year. 1967 — the one-hundredth anniversary of the Confederation of Upper and Lower Canada and two of the Maritime provinces. In 1867 it had been a unique event. This cold night it was an event worth celebrating. The ninety-ninth year did not appear to be anything special. The one-hundred-and-first year would be business as usual. But the hundredth year! Anything but usual.

Seconds after the Peace Tower clock booms nine,* the all-dressed-up prime minister and his secretary of state breathe sighs of relief, leave their seats in the deep freeze and stroll to a low 6-foot-wide octagonal structure 160 feet closer to Wellington Street on the main north-south axis of the Parliament Buildings. The equally relieved dignitaries follow, stamping their feet and hugging themselves with exaggerated gestures to get the circulation going.

The structure housed a jet fuelled by natural gas, whose inert hydrocarbon molecules have travelled through a pipeline 2,500 miles east from Alberta. These molecules are soon to become excited. The first flicker of the Centennial flame.

Mr. Pearson applies the torch. Flame issues forth, the Centennial choir bursts into "O Canada" in both official languages and thus occurs the first symbolic event in 1967 in Canada. The year would see an unprecedented and unexpected series of programs, projects and festivities — a cavalcade that would change Canada and its people. Positive and benevolent, the Centennial celebrations would prove to be a model of how a mega-anniversary should be conducted. An example of the finest kind of impetus affirming and encouraging peaceful societal evolution.

---

* Midnight would have been better, but the children in the choir had to get home to bed. In any case, considering Canada's 5 1/2 time zones, it was an acceptable compromise.

By the time the Earth had completed one more revolution around the sun and 1968 had arrived, the Centennial flame was still burning. Officials felt compelled to chronicle all that had happened but the compulsion to celebrate had dissipated. Something of the spirit of the biographer prevailed, who wrote, "Ne'er of the living shall the living judge. Too short the memory. Too deep the grudge." The official retrospective was never undertaken. The only *post facto* piece to appear was one written by Judy LaMarsh in the lively chronicle of her outstanding career, *Memoirs of a Bird in a Gilded Cage,* published in 1969. She devoted the longest of eleven sizzling chapters to "Centennial Summer." Hers is a fascinating minister's eye-view of the year 1967 itself — an anecdotal, forgivably self-serving and sometimes inaccurate account, but eminently readable.

There was as well an elegant coffee table book, *Canada '67 The Best of Centennial in Pictures,* produced by the Centennial Commission and published by the Queen's Printer in 1968. The text was written by Blair Fraser, long-time Ottawa correspondent for *Maclean's* magazine, and Jean-Marc Poliquin, a CBC staffer and member of the Parliamentary Press Gallery. The 180-page, 16-inch by 12-inch book was a reasonable pictorial record of Centennial year but did not attempt any analysis or provide any detailed description.

What follows is another kind of story. It is an attempt on the part of a working stiff, one who was in on the planning, preparations and operations from start to finish, to relate what happened. But it is more than that. It is also an attempt to discover why people seem compelled to celebrate certain anniversaries.

By offering an insider's view of the personnel and organizational machinery that went into the Centennial celebrations, I hope to provide other anniversary planners with a sense of successes to imitate and pitfalls to avoid — a recipe for the successful observance of an anniversary. As the year 2000 approaches and we move into the Third Millenium of the Christian Era, nations all around the world will be looking to planners to come up with ideas for an appropriate celebration.

Among those who will find this book useful are:

- Politicians and officials of all member countries of the United Nations
- International public servants
- Leaders of non-government international organizations
- Administrators of universities and other institutions of higher learning
- Any individual, group, corporation or other entity who might be planning large anniversary celebrations of any sort.

The style is anecdotal more than analytical, since this account of the Centennial celebrations is also a memoir. Others might have written a different memoir. This is my perspective. My story. But beyond the memoir there is much to be learned by example, and planners of future celebrations will be able to apply the lessons we learned to their planning activities.

Since anniversaries mark the passage of history and are part of history themselves, I have devoted one chapter to an overview of the historical events surrounding Canada's birth as a modern political state. Another chapter provides a brief description of the social and political climate that prevailed before and during the Centennial year.

For readers unfamiliar with Canadian history, these descriptions should help put the Centennial celebrations in context. For Canadians, they will serve as a reminder of who we are and what exactly we were celebrating back in '67. Throughout these chapters, there will also be some emphasis on Quebec's attitude to Confederation and its sense of identity within Canada.

As in any family, the individual "members" of a country sometimes have grievances against each other, and the provinces of Canada are no exception. Since Confederation, Quebec has rarely felt completely comfortable within the Canadian embrace.

Anniversaries can increase divisions like this or heal them to some extent. Published at a time when Canada is in the midst of restructuring its political edifice to accommodate the disparate wishes of its provinces, this book may shed a shaft of light on how the Centennial celebrations of 1967 healed or failed to heal divisions.

Just as it took seven years to refine the concept, structure, process and procedures of Centennial year, this book has been published in time for individuals, institutions, voluntary agencies and nation states to take note when they feel the compulsion to do something about the turn of the century. Something special. A special *fin de siècle*.

Once in a thousand years.

The Centennial flame still burns to this day, shut down only twice a year for cleaning and to remove the hope-coins tossed into its watery basin.* For the elemental flame of fire is a regenerating fountain.

It will no doubt still be burning as we approach and pass the year 2000. Hold your breath for the biggest celebration the global village has ever seen.

---

* Public Works Canada turns them over to the Receiver General of Canada (the deputy minister of Supply and Services Canada), and they become a credit to the Consolidated Revenue Fund, from whence they are distributed to charitable organizations. About a thousand dollars a year are involved in this act of high finance.

1

The Anniversary Compulsion

O N THAT DEEP-FROZEN New Year's Eve back in 1966, it is doubtful that anyone was asking themselves why they were celebrating their country's hundredth anniversary. What do you mean "Why" they would have responded if they'd been asked. It's just something you do every ten, twenty-five, or hundred years to honour your country. The band players and the dignitaries, the ordinary onlookers and the members of the choir had more in common than frost-bitten toes. In a country not noted for blowing its own horn, they were enjoying a rare moment of national pride.

Not that it was really their business to wonder. An anniversary, after all, is a time to celebrate, not a sociology class. So it is hardly surprising that the Canadian public sat back and soaked up their Centennial festivities with no second thoughts. That's what they were supposed to do!

But what of the Centennial mandarins and workhorses — the powers-that-were and the people behind the scenes who spent months and years putting the show together? Surely they would have set themselves some objectives right at the beginning. Surely they would have asked why all the fuss, why all the expenditure of energy and money. These are the questions most planners ask.

The truth is, they didn't ask these questions — or if they did, it was only for a few fleeting moments between planning meetings and purchase orders. No one stopped to ask why we were celebrating. It was like a categorical imperative. You just did it. That's all.

As director of special projects for the Centennial Commission, and a member of its Management Committee, I had partial responsibility for determining *how* we were going to celebrate the Centennial but when I thought about *why* we were celebrating, I did not get beyond the stage of amateur musings. And no one else seemed to be asking the question. There was no one with whom I could engage in dialogue. I sensed that the phenomenon at hand was in the field of social psychology, but nowhere in our range of advisors was there a social psychologist to be found.

The closest I came was in conversation with a sociology professor at the University of New Brunswick during negotiations for the participation of the province in Centennial programs. Sitting in the Faculty Club on their seven-thousand-acre campus, the prof said he recognized the import of my question but had no clear answer. He did say, however, "The last thing you should give a retiree on his sixty-fifth birthday is a watch, gold or otherwise. He doesn't want to be reminded of the passage of time. That's cruel. Give him a down payment on a sports car!"

In other words, the celebration should fit the audience, as well as the occasion. The planners should think about how their programs and awards will make people feel.

The Centennial program was designed without such an analysis. Perhaps we met the societal need without understanding that there was a need or what shape and dimensions it had. The new governments in Eastern Europe are being run by playwrights and history professors. When they are catapulted into an anniversary, will these scholarly leaders search for philosophical meaning? What will they find? Will it make a difference in the design of the program?

It quite likely would make a difference. Most of Canada's Centennial celebrations were resounding successes. Others were weak in their impact. Some did not seem to belong at all. There is no guarantee that our successes would have been greater if we had first asked ourselves why we were celebrating, but it might have helped.

What I discovered during the course of subsequent research is that there is a lack of any academic study that deals specifically with the topic of anniversaries. I found material dealing with a variety of associated themes: rites and rituals, myths and customs, symbol theory, mass psychology and organizational behaviour. It became clear that a comprehensive analysis of this material was required. And it did not exist. Here is a fascinating cultural studies topic waiting to be explored.

This chapter reviews what academic materials I have found, summarizes my own experience in Canada and concludes with a summary of the considerations the planners of mega-anniversaries should keep in mind.

What we are dealing with lies principally in the field of anthropology. Specifically, it is linked with rite, ritual, ceremony and custom. According to the *International Encyclopedia of the Social Sciences,* "since the 14th Century those terms have been used interchangeably to denote any non-instinctive predictable action or series of actions that cannot be justified by a 'rational', means-to-ends type of explanation."

I had wondered whether the compulsion to celebrate recurrent calendric dates was encoded in our genes like the survival instinct, but apparently this is going too far. According to the scholars consulted, rituals and customs are not facts of nature, but concepts, and there is a lot of overlap between the terms used to describe anniversary celebrations.

In the *Encyclopedia of the Social Sciences,* Edmund R. Leach writes: "Even among those who have specialized in this field, there is the widest possible disagreement as to how the word *ritual* should be used and how the performance of ritual should be understood." James Frazer agrees. In his great classic, *The Golden Bough,* he uses *custom, ceremonial, rite* and *ritual* interchangeably. So take your pick. I will stay with *rite* and *ritual,* since I believe the observance of anniversaries to be ritual behaviour.

A ritual is a technical act that *does* something. But it is also a communicative act that *says* something. Shaking hands is a ritual. It says, "I'm glad to meet you. Let's converse."

At the group level, ritual serves to remind a group just where each member stands in relation to every other and in relation to a larger system. It is necessary to have those occasional reminders. It is reassuring.

Consider the Roman Catholic Mass. The Mass is a ritual. Within it are ceremonial aspects, the vestures of the priest, the singing, chanting and scripture reading, communion, and all is a celebration. Church rhetoric speaks of the "celebration of mass."

Jane E. Harrison, in her book *Ancient Art and Ritual,* states that "primitive man tends to re-enact whatever makes him feel strongly, any one of his manifestations, hunting, fighting, ploughing, sowing, provided it be of sufficient interest and importance, is material for a rite." She further claims that "the performances of ritual generate in the act certain sentiments that are advantageous to the society as a whole" — as hunting, ploughing and sowing always are and fighting sometimes is.

This leads to another concept related to anniversaries: rites of passage. At the individual level, people of all cultures celebrate or mark certain times of transition in their own lives as well as in the lives of members of their family and perhaps close friends. Birth, puberty, marriage and death have been celebrated in a variety of rituals and ceremonies. Similarly, on a collective level, communities and societies celebrate the passing of time by the members reassuring each other of the value and worth of their shared history.

This type of reassurance is sought in recurrent calendric ceremonies such as birthdays and New Year's Day. Similarly, wedding anniversaries are recognized at the tenth, twenty-fifth, and fiftieth years. This is tradition. It is predictable. The steps taken to celebrate such birthdays and wedding anniversaries occur within families. The events are family-specific and they are mandatory. The family is compelled to do it. They feel they have no choice. When a couple has been married fifty years, in essence the significant thing is that they have stayed alive and been together for that long period. A period, as we measure the passage of time, that is even, neatly configured and ends in zero. Or put another way, it is neatly divisible by five. It is really a milestone in their passage — a milestone that is placed arbitrarily, but is recognizable.

The milestone is viewed differently by the different parties affected. The couple's children want to recognize the date and do something about it. Rarely will the golden anniverserants plan their own party. Those persons slightly removed from the parties who are the immediate focus of attention look on it as a celebration, a time of ceremonies, festivities and the bestowing of honours, by way of speeches and perhaps gifts. And as Jane Harrison has noted, the feelings of assurance generated by the celebration contribute to the well-being of those who are being celebrated.

The compulsion to mark mega-anniversaries of institutions and legally constituted cities, states and nations is of a different order. But it too is mandatory, not permissive. One day, someplace, in one person's mind, the thought occurs:

"Something ought to be done."

Centennial celebrations are national anniversaries that allow the participants to deal with such questions as who they are and how they feel about themselves, to emphasize their similarities and minimize their differences. Not unlike human birthdays, national birthdays symbolize not only birth and the passage of time, but also achievement and growth — reminding people of the past that shapes their present.

Lloyd Warner's studies of the symbolic life of Americans deals directly with the symbols of history as presented in national or community celebrations. "All societies uphold and reaffirm at regular intervals the collective sentiments and collective ideas which help to maintain their unity. History is not presented in a purely objective way but reflects contemporary expectations that have often revalued and reconceptualized historical meaning. In many respects it is part of the role of the commemorative celebration to use the past to express present values; to successfully integrate the past into the present. In this way national or community celebrations are organized to reaffirm the social structure of the country or community. Warner argues that such secular celebrations allow people to collectively "worship their own images and achievements; their own since they were made by themselves and fashioned from their experiences among themselves."

Another more recent anthropologist, Victor Turner, argues that people in all cultures recognize the need to set aside certain times and spaces for celebratory use. He suggests that just as psychologists consider the capacity to dream to be indispensable for mental health, so the ability to be exposed to the objectified dreams thrown up by the enthusiasm of celebration may be necessary for social health. "We confront our own personal, singular depths more fully in these collective forms than we do through introspection, for they arise from a heightened sense of our shared humanity." When a nation celebrates an event, it is also celebrating itself; "it attempts to manifest, in symbolic form, what it conceives to be its essential life, at once the distillation and typification of its corporate experience."

Turner argues that celebrating the passage of time incorporates aspects from the celebration of rites of passage and seasonal festivals in that it provides an organizing set of principles, traditional ways of binding opposing forces in the community and tying together the past with the present.

Anthropologists studying cultural performances have compiled some interesting work on celebration. Among them, a Canadian book of essays entitled *The Celebration of Society: Perspectives on Contemporary Cultural Performance* edited by Frank Manning. In this volume Manning examines the significance of celebration in sociopolitical processes. He argues that celebration is performance, in that it is a dramatic presentation of cultural symbols; it is entertainment, regardless of ideological significance or intent; it is public, in that it socializes personal meanings; and it is participatory, not a show for disengaged visitors.

Manning points out that in industrialized societies, celebrations have a strong ritual component. When those who control celebration also dominate the social order, that dominance also becomes part of the ritual. Play, on the other hand, predominates in celebrations of more traditional societies, or among minorities within industrialized societies, where the organizers are in a subordinate position.

Carole Farber's article, "High, Healthy, and Happy: Ontario Mythology on Parade," included in Manning's book, approaches the town celebration as a "rite of passage" in that it acts to give members of the community a secure sense of their inherited culture. Celebrations become occasions "when cultural and national identity can be reasserted and feelings of self-awareness and participation in common experiences reaffirmed."

In his analysis of the rites of passage, social psychologist W.S.F. Pickering examines various findings connecting "rites" with occasions that bring with them fear and anxiety, where individuals seek a process, often involving family members and close friends, to help them deal with uncertainty. Arguably, larger occasions that affect a wider group of people, such as a centenary or millennium, also serve to allay fear and uncertainty regarding the future and the direction the nation or world is heading. Pickering adds a note of caution, however: anthropological explanations of the human need for ritual derived from the study of primitive societies are not necessarily applicable to modern ones. He argues that modern society is more educated, has more freedom and is less compelled to accept ritual; the need is for ceremony not ritual. Although the dictionary definitions of the two terms read like synonyms of each other, *ceremony* has the implication of a secular non-spiritual event while *ritual* has the connotation of a spiritual, religious, pagan or magical event.

Roger Abrahams, in "The Language of Festivals," focuses on celebration as the time people set aside for play and pleasure. He argues that during times of celebration, fun which is associated with deep human feelings is disengaged from people's day-to-day anxieties. "Festive occasions continue to draw on these most archaic and basic motives and means of having fun seriously...[We] celebrate nothing less than the continuity and vitality of humans in groups." Turner would agree, recognizing that, although humankind has a need for order, there exists an equivalent need for the arousal, heightened activity and emotional responsiveness experienced in celebration. He points out that humans are festive creatures and that the festive spirit is rooted deep in history, in the form of pageantry and ceremony.

In *Fairs and Festivals*, Richard Chase examines the historical role of festivals and fairs and argues that they provide tangible exhibits of the important aspects of a culture or society. In his view, the community festival is unique in that it reminds each person that he or she is a member of a particular group — and this often counteracts some of the more alienating trends of modern life, such as rootlessness, mobility and loss of identification in mainstream society.

Archaeologist Lucia Nixon, in analyzing rites of passage, stated in an article in *The Ottawa Citizen*: "When people in a particular group engage in ritual behavior they transmit information to themselves and to each other about their current state of being..., it is often a symbolic restatement of beliefs and social relationships... ."

Thus it appears that the anniversary compulsion is rooted in a basic, profound psychic need for reassurance and reaffirmation, for continuity and restatement and in the need to counteract alienating trends. If the milestone in our passage through time, when divided by five, ends in a zero or five, the program kicks in. Why five? Five fingers? Five toes? Five senses? Five continents?

One accepted meaning of the word *passage* is a journey or a voyage. If we accept time as something we pass through, rather than something that passes, as in *tempus fugit*, we have a useful construct to help us understand the significance and impact of anniversaries.

Consider life as a voyage or a journey. We pass through time and reach a five-year milestone or a twenty-five-year milestone. When we arrive at each one, we need to stop and recognize that we have journeyed that far. Our arrival calls for a prescribed act or a solemn ceremony. It calls for a rite of passage. As this analysis has tried to indicate, milestones and the rites they engender satisfy deeply felt, possibly unrecognized psychic needs in the journey through time of individuals, tribes, villages, communities, cities, regions, organizations and nation states.

Identity is affirmed when we pause to recognize achievements and growth. By viewing and reviewing how past experiences have shaped present values, subtle psychic needs are satisfied, and individual mental health and group social health are strengthened. We develop a measure of confidence and certainty about the next incremental step in our voyage. Look from whence we have come! Look toward where we are evolving! Where the milestone being observed is a shared experience of aggregations of humans all the way from tribes to nation states, a unifying force is felt. We have all done this! Look what we have accomplished in common! Further, should there be destructive forces at work, the celebration of our common experience tends to oppose those forces.

While individuals may not realize they have psychic needs that can be assuaged at anniversary time, and while nation states may not notice the needy nature of the *polis*, one inescapable fact cannot be denied. The milestone is there. It won't go away. Individuals can try to ignore it or adopt a blasé attitude, but in doing so, positive incremental growth is being denied. Similarly, organizations and nation states can ignore an anniversary but at the risk of losing a unique opportunity to consolidate, strengthen and expand the corporate well-being. By celebrating anniversaries, whether we realize it or not, we are making a positive incremental contribution to our evolution — "the development or growth according to its inherent tendencies of anything that can be compared to a living organism."

My motivation in getting involved with Centennial activities was fuelled by the hope that Canada and Canadians would grow a little. It is generally acknowledged that we did.

Following Centennial year I was recruited into the Privy Council Office and became an active participant in the Priorities and Planning Secretariat, where I observed an experience germane to this analysis. It was this. Prime Minister Trudeau had surrounded himself with bright young planners with management skills and analytical minds. In setting the goals for his first administration (1968-73), Trudeau realized that the things the government wanted to do were directly related to the values the government held. The language of the day was that norms derived from values in the same way that ethics derive from morals. You behave in a certain way because of what you believe. The Cabinet couldn't come up with a list of values, so we looked at all the Cabinet decisions of the previous administration and the new administration to date and presented them with a chart. They saw a list of their decisions and a list of the values they must have held to make those decisions. Once they knew their collective values, they could develop programs that reflected those values. They backed into thinking about why they were doing things.

In concluding this chapter I wanted to develop a set of principles that planners could use to create successful anniversary celebrations. Since no one gave much thought to the philosophy behind the celebrations that took place in 1967, no list of governing "values" was ever drawn up. Like the Cabinet example above I reasoned that the Canadian organism intuitively did certain things in response to the rite of passage, thus revealing additional phenomena that went beyond what the academics cited consider to be normal anniversary ritual.

So in this book I developed a framework of my own — combining some of the ideas of the scholars mentioned earlier in this chapter with observations I made about the successes and failures of programs and events that actually took place during the Centennial year. As a practical convenience I wanted to reduce the set of principles, the framework, to some handy form. *The Anniversary Axiomatique* on the next page is what I finally came up with. A set of rules for anniversary planners.

THE ANNIVERSARY AXIOMATIQUE

1. Reinforce the identity of the organism: in doing this, spend lots of time understanding all the dimensions of that identity.

2. Provide continuity and restatement, reminding people of the past that shapes the present: reassure the people of the value and worth of shared history by recognizing achievement and growth.

3. Seek out and accentuate unifying elements: symbols, songs and all things that are held in common, that have bonding potential.

4. Analyze destructive forces that may be present: thoughtfully plan how to aggressively oppose them.

5. Focus some part of the program on the future: give people confidence and determination to continue the voyage.

6. Encourage personal and community improvement: like when a special visitor is expected in the home, everyone wants to do their best and look their best.

7. Build monuments and memorials: these are tangible statements of achievement and strong elements of a sense of continuity.

8. Give gifts: not commodities that have only commercial value but gifts that keep on giving, gifts that have expanding worth.

9. Set up performances and public events and encourage participation: it is in sharing with others at the same time and place the experience of large-scale spectacles that one feels warmth, and pride and cohesion.

10. Make sure it's fun, but also allow for dignity and emotion: it is healthy to release the spirit through noise, through laughter, through tears and through awe.

If you follow these precepts, it is axiomatic that what you do in ritual response to the anniversary compulsion will be positive and evolutionary, benevolent and full of pleasant memories.

Read on and see how *The Anniversary Axiomatique* played out in practice as Canada and Canadians responded to their big anniversary in 1967.

CHAPTER 2

History

T HE IDENTITY OF AN INDIVIDUAL comprises many elements. Where you came from. How you got there. What you have accomplished. What you possess. What you believe. All are implicitly included as components of a general statement, "I am ... ." The same applies to countries. Where a country came from is a strong determinant (but not the only one) of identity.

In order to tailor anniversary programs to a nation's identity, it is essential to look to the past. Canada's Centennial planners did not do this in a systematic way, although their sense of the country's collective history strongly coloured the development of some of the most successful Centennial manifestations.

Before I go on to describe these and other programs and festivities, I would like to pause for a moment and glance back at Canada's past — to help you understand the events that shaped the Canadian psyche and to give a sense of the kind of historical analysis you should undertake before you begin your megaplans. In the next chapter, I will look briefly at domestic political events that were happening at the time of the Centennial celebrations, for these also helped determine the country's sense of identity and created issues that the Centennial celebrations might have addressed more successfully.

To begin, however, let's take a glance back at the past.

The story of Canadian Confederation is primarily about politics, and by definition, about politicians. It is also about the predominant brands of religion at the time — the Roman Catholic and the Protestant. And of course it is about real flesh-and-blood people whose emotions were the same as ours. They experienced loneliness, fear, anger, pride, contentment. The physical context in which they lived was different and would appear strange to us, but their mental abilities and spiritual yearnings were just like ours.

In days gone by, religion and politics were two taboo subjects in polite conversation. Yet these two themes, along with the third taboo subject, sex, are universal phenomena that exist in every place and time. That is why they are fundamental to Canada's history. Of course, not much has been recorded about sex. Confederation happened in Victorian times, and it's generally acknowledged that there was a lot going on, but not much was written about it. Certainly not much about Confederation-era politicians, despite the flesh-and-blood real live humans that they and their ladies were.

The Confederation story is more. It's about war, assassination, racism. It's about economics and capitalism. And it's about statesmanship. And at more than one important phase it is about that great lubricant, the active ingredient that was discovered thousands of years ago from honey left too long in the pot. Booze.

One aspect of the story, which surfaces again and again, almost as a subplot, is the role played by French Canada and by Canadians of French origin. These were the original Canadians, called that by the aboriginal people who gave them the name "people who live in huts." In French it is *Canadiens*, and they started as New France in 1610, many, many generations before the English took over as conquerors in 1759.

Their survival in a new land, their accommodation to the role of a vanquished people, and their stubborn efforts to retain and maintain their uniqueness, have strongly influenced Canadian history. Consideration of the ethos of the modern Quebec and its people, direct descendants of *les Canadiens*, was a major determinant in planning the celebration of the one-hundred-year milestone marking the date that put them in a political federation with the British colonies in North America. The subjective sense of nationalism, nationhood and nation is a profound reality in Quebec, peaking again at the time of writing, as it has done repeatedly since the Conquest of 1759. This reality has sometimes been recognized and sometimes been ignored by the Canadian governing bodies. The Centennial planners, likewise, dealt with this issue with mixed success.

The part of the North American continent that was known as British North America in the mid-nineteenth century had five components: the Province of Canada, a legislative union of Canada East and Canada West (consisting of smaller versions of present-day Ontario and Quebec); the provinces of New Brunswick and Nova Scotia; and the two island colonies, Prince Edward Island and Newfoundland. To the west of the Province of Canada was a vast stretch of territory that was largely unsettled, and while officially owned by the British Crown, most of it was leased to the British-based Hudson's Bay Company, the fur-trading monolithic *extraordinaire*. The only settled parts were the colony of Vancouver Island, created in 1849, and a settlement dating from 1811, known as Red River, at the junction of the Red and Assiniboine Rivers. Expansion westward in the United States had proceeded more swiftly. While the United States stretched from sea to sea by 1867, Canada wasn't even halfway there.

The union between Canada East (Quebec) and Canada West (Ontario) proved to be too restrictive for the youthful society of Canada West. Its wishes could easily be thwarted by the block of Canada East assemblymen, who often represented interests at variance with those of Canada West. But by 1851 Canada West had numerical advantage over Canada East and raised the cry for representation by population. They were led by the reformer George Brown, publisher of the Toronto *Globe*, a liberal newspaper. Needless to say, "rep by pop" was vehemently opposed by Canada East. Equal representation was an essential guarantee of their French identity and interests, which they defended at all levels; it was essential to *survivance*, survival in the face of all opposing forces.

Settlement of the West was feared by the French Canadian leaders in Lower Canada. They reasoned that a colonized West could become a political adjunct to the Canada West block in the Assembly, thus weakening their position, especially if rep by pop were instituted. In the course of the conflict between the two groups, racism raised its unpretty and durable head. Hear the *Globe* in 1863:

> ...we urge that every opportunity may be given for the just settlement of the Representation question, and the opening of the great Northwest,
>
> ...we don't want to see Canada financially ruined. We do not want to see her progress hindered by the continued domination of a power the highest of whose aspirations is the conservation of everything French.

Dissension was heightened when the Assembly's French Canadian Catholic majority succeeded in legislating a separate parallel system of primary Roman Catholic schools throughout Canada East and Canada West. Canada West's largely Protestant population held ancient prejudices against the Catholics and also felt that this was bound to dilute the amount of funds available to the regular school system. The separate school legislation so resented at the time exists to this very day, providing two school systems in Ontario.

By the early 1860s the parties were evenly balanced in the Legislative Assembly, and had become rigidly polarized. Executive government became impossible. Radical constitutional change had become essential.

These were the internal forces, but the Province of Canada and the colonies and scattered settlements of British North America at the time were not a closed system. They were greatly influenced by external attitudes, perceptions and actions which eventually played a major role in the creation of the political structure called Confederation. The external forces came from the United States and Britain.

The United States had agreed in 1854 to eliminate tariff barriers on goods and services entering the United States from the British North American colonies. British North America returned the favour. The Reciprocity Treaty that legally established this arrangement was due to expire in 1866, and the Americans stated their intention to abrogate it. This meant that impossibly high artificial tariff walls would be erected and Canada's surplus coal, fish, farm and forest products would be rejected by the U.S. market in favour of lower-priced American products.

Securing another market or an expanded market would be essential. The most logical one would be an east-west-shaped market, and it could be created only through the union of the colonies and the expansion of Canada to the west, ideally all the way to the Pacific.

This protectionist attitude was related to the Civil War. Britain had declared neutrality at the beginning of the five-year cataclysmic conflict, but in actual practice, she sympathized with the southern Confederate states. A succession of incidents and escapades, many of them resulting from the activities of Confederate sympathizers based in Canada, produced continuous tension between the United States and Great Britain. The North hardened its posture toward Great Britain and her colonies in North America, and Secretary of State Seward ordered the border states to fortify themselves against the eventuality of a foreign attack. The possible threat from south of the border drew Britain's attention to the need for defence and for consistent railway service. Railway interests also played a part in the creation of Canada. In the mid-nineteenth century, fifteen hundred miles of railway were scattered between Lake Huron and the Atlantic coast, but many of the owners of the track were in financial difficulties. These private sector interests believed they would flourish if a railway were to eventually stretch from the Atlantic to the Pacific. The union of the colonies could provide a base for such a move. The railway itself would have to be financed by external capital. British capital.

Other forces were in play which heightened Britain's interest in its colony. One was avaricious thoughts on the part of the

Americans about occupying the west, especially the Red River Valley (in present-day Manitoba) and the Pacific Northwest (in present-day British Columbia). Another was the Fenian Movement. The Fenians Brotherhood, created by the Irish of New York City as an instrument for the independence of Ireland, announced its intention of striking at Britain through her vulnerable North American possessions. There were rumours that the Fenians, many of them veterans of the Union army, disbanded since the Civil War, were massing along the American border in the spring of 1866. The Fenians launched a fifteen-hundred-man invasion of the Niagara Peninsula in June and made a foray into the Eastern Townships the same year. But it was in New Brunswick that they played a catalytic role in the march toward Confederation. There they assembled a large force on the shores of Passamoquody Bay, intent on invasion, and some actually occupied Montebello Island for a short period before being driven back to Maine by British regulars who rushed in to meet the threat.

While the Province of Canada in the early 1860s recognized that structural change was needed, the prevailing attitude in the four Atlantic provinces was totally different. The idea of a legislative union of British North America had no appeal. They all enjoyed commercial prosperity based on overseas trade with Britain and the United States and looked out across the ocean, rather than inward to the interior. They had no internal problems to make them long for political reorganization.

There was, however, a mild interest in some kind of Maritime union. Each province was small and weak and incapable of any great action on its own. This idea was promoted by successive lieutenant-governors of New Brunswick and Nova Scotia. Samuel Leonard Tilley, the chief minister of New Brunswick, and Charles Tupper, the leader of the Nova Scotia government, were both able to summon a degree of support for the plan.

Prince Edward Island showed no interest in a union. Newfoundland's interest was even weaker. After all, one of their renowned folk songs included the lines,

Our face is to England
Our back to the Gulf
Stay away at your peril
Canadian wolf.

The lyrics were an accurate reflection of the prevailing attitude in what was to become Canada's easternmost province.
In 1864, resolutions were passed in the Maritime provinces
favouring a conference on union. If it were to be held it had
to be in Charlottetown, the consensus on the mainland being
that no Prince Edward Island delegation would leave the
island. That would be showing too much interest, academic or
otherwise.

In other words, although some governing bodies were far
from committed to the idea of union, many recognized that
major structural change was required. The initiative for union,
however, came almost exclusively from government and not
from the population at large. As Canadian historian Donald
Swainson has put it:

There was no broad movement for any single programme of
change and an attempt to create such a movement would have
failed. Thus the political leaders were required to work out a
new settlement and to impose it on the populace without
recourse to a referendum or a general election in each of the
colonies. This point was well expressed by L.B. Irwin, an
American historian. He explained that "The Confederation movement...was not a spontaneous action of the people demanding
national unity. Rather it was a deliberate move of the controlling
statesmen to protect the people against dangers that many of
them did not recognize or fear." Thus the Confederation movement was *non*-popular in the sense that it was not the product
of a mass movement, and *un*popular in the sense that various
parts of the settlement were disliked by various components of
the federation. Both the non-popular and the unpopular aspects
of Confederation were inevitable once it was decided to include
in one union Canada, New Brunswick, Nova Scotia, Prince
Edward Island and the Northwest. These units were so disparate

in nature as to make popular consensus impossible and the concept of a single popular movement, absurd.

The trend toward union led to two historic conferences in 1864, the Charlottetown Conference and the Quebec Conference. Each was in its own way a preparatory and creative happening that shaped the mould from which a new federal state in North America would be cast on July 1, 1867.

Meanwhile a political phenomenon was occurring in the Province of Canada that has become known as the Great Coalition. The polarization between Canada East and Canada West had led to total constipation, and George Brown had made arrangements for the appointment of a select committee of the Assembly to inquire into the situation. When it finished its work the committee reported "a strong feeling in favour of changes in the direction of a Federal system."

Brown initiated conversations with his political opponents in both Canada West and Canada East and won a pledge from his own party and the three other parties to form a coalition to work together to bring in a federal system for Canada. The Cabinet was re-jigged to permit participation of the various party representatives. John A. Macdonald of Canada West and George-Étienne Cartier of Canada East gave up their formal designations as leaders of the two Canadas, George Brown, the opposition leader in Canada West, joined the inner circle and Sir Étienne-Paschal Taché became the titular prime minister. Cartier saw in a federal system the potential for protecting French Canadians' rights, especially if he could have a hand in enshrining those rights into the system's constitution. Macdonald was passionately devoted to the federal concept, thinking he could engineer a strong central government; Brown was a reformer, and felt that federation was a long-overdue reform. Taché was an obliging figurehead.

Confederation was not universally popular in Quebec, since it was viewed as a possible threat to French language and customs and to the existence of separate schools. (The hard-won legislation allowing for such schools might be reversed in the new federation.) Cartier's French Canadian supporters realized, too, that they would definitely end up as a minority. The coalition carried risk to political careers and Cartier and all the others entered into it with this knowledge.

It is extremely difficult in any society to find politicians willing to give up something for the common good. To get them to step aside, to give up power voluntarily, to openly acknowledge the superiority of a person other than themselves is a rare occurrence. In 1864, the participants in the Great Coalition transcended politics and acted like statesmen.

A conference to discuss Maritime union was set for September 1, 1864, in Charlottetown, to which the Canadians would try to wangle an invitation to attend as observers.

Meanwhile, others had been working behind the scenes to woo the Maritimes into a wider union. Before the formation of the Great Coalition, Thomas D'Arcy McGee (one of Macdonald's Cabinet ministers who was assassinated in Ottawa on April 7, 1868) and others like-minded who sensed a new era was dawning and that Maritime politicians might need courting, with the complicity of the Saint John Board of Trade, had set up a kind of excursion to the Maritimes for interested parties. Just a social thing spurred by the new talk of Confederation. The organizers received an enthusiastic response: the group who eventually signed up included twenty-three newspaper editors and correspondents, eighteen members of the Legislative Council (the executive group), thirty-two from the Assembly (the larger legislation group) and a number of private individuals. About one hundred people altogether.

The cruise down the St. Lawrence was romantic. The late summer days and nights were balmy, the shipboard passengers relaxed. Conversation was non-partisan for the moment; there would be plenty of time for political talk later. As they docked at Saint John, the passengers were astonished by a crowd estimated at ten thousand people cheering and waving them in. It was party time: official dinners, boat trips, spontaneous sing-songs, military bands on parade. At one stop on a one-day boat trip, as tribute to the French Canadians on board, one-quarter of the Canadian party, a banner appeared declaring, *"Vive les Canadiens!"*

Here were British subjects in British North America who did not know each other. The get-together was developing into a family reunion where distant cousins meet for the first time and discover each other's merit. But the people at this unique affair were more than cousins. They were brothers and sisters. The mystical, yet practical, tie that bound them all was the British monarch and the monarchy. What appeared to prevail was goodwill and a willingness to work together.

The overtures made at high political levels to attend the Charlottetown conference for Maritime union were successful. On Monday, August 29, early in the evening, the Canadian government steamer *Victoria* sailed from Quebec for Charlottetown. Two-thirds of the Cabinet were on board. For a month, they had been preparing their scheme of union. On September 1, the impressive man-of-war-like *Victoria* put into harbour and the delegates, impeccably attired, were rowed ashore in two boats, each with four oarsmen and boatsmen in blue uniforms. A most impressive group of "observers," arriving in a most impressive manner.

At the Conference which started that afternoon with non-substantive pleasantries in the graceful Georgian Province House, it was decided to give the floor to the Canadians, probably as a courtesy, but possibly because the Prince Edward Island delegates didn't think Maritime union was going anywhere, so it didn't matter who spoke first.

The next morning and on succeeding days the well-thought-out scheme of Confederation was laid out — by John A. Macdonald, George-Étienne Cartier, George Brown and Alexander Tilloch Galt, the Montreal entrepreneurial politician whose consuming interest was railway construction. The proposed structure was described, the division of powers, financial and judicial details. The closed-door meetings were interspersed with good fellowship and good drinks. (In the hold of the *Victoria*, a stock of boxes of French champagne had been securely lashed, and the crew was kept busy bringing it ashore, bottles to be popped at every opportunity.)

The great lubricator played a major role in loosening tongues, promoting uninhibited conversation and causing smiles and laughter. It was like one long cocktail party that went on for days and days. On one occasion, according to Maritime historian P.B. Waite, someone rose and called to attention the crowd and published there and then the banns of marriage between the colonies. In time they would come down from their euphoria. There would be hangovers, both physical and political, but the colonies would never be the same. This Conference was changing things.

The original purpose of the Conference on Maritime Union got lost in the shuffle, but as P.B. Waite puts it, "...the conference gave Confederation in the Maritimes something of the impetus it already had in Canada. More important it gave the delegates themselves a sense of common destiny, a devotion to a cause greater than their old local loyalties; indeed, it swept some delegates out of their insular identities altogether." As had happened in the Great Coalition, individuals were willing to give something up for the common good. There was indeed running at the time "a tide in the affairs of men."

The fortune toward which it all led was a transcontinental national identity — and the eventual formation of the Dominion of Canada.

THE QUEBEC CONFERENCE

John A. Macdonald lost no time in getting Governor General Charles Stanley Monck to call for the appointment of delegates from the three maritime provinces and Newfoundland to meet with the Canadian Cabinet at Quebec on October 10. No further preliminary discussions were necessary because he had the whole scheme of Confederation reduced to writing and in his back pocket before he left Charlottetown — ready to strike while the iron was hot.

The conference took place in an unpretentious brick building on the site now occupied by the present Château

Frontenac, overlooking the St. Lawrence River. (Its three large Romanesque windows form the background for the famous painting of the assembled delegates known as the *Fathers of Confederation,* executed by Robert Harris.) Of the delegates from each province, except in the case of New Brunswick, the majority were Conservatives. The chairman was the ninety-year-old patriarchal Sir Étienne-Paschal Taché, but Macdonald dominated the meeting. He was a monarchist, fearful of the threat of the Americans and in favour of a strong central government. The seventy-two resolutions of the Conference pointed to a high degree of central control.

Many of the delegates were of Scottish origin, and while most of these had been born in Scotland, not one of the French Canadians had been born in France. They and their ancestors had been *Canadiens* for six generations. Yet, the Conference proceedings were carried out entirely in English! Of the thirty-three delegates who met at Quebec, only four were French Canadian: George-Étienne Cartier, Jean-Charles Chapais, Hector-Louis Langevin and Antoine-Aimé Dorion, who had until then energetically opposed Confederation. This time around, however, he and the other French Canadian delegates appear to have remained remarkably silent. It can be speculated that they were co-operating with the inevitable.

The French Canadians got the right to retain their Napoleonic *code civile* for civil law, the use of French in the courts, in the legislature and also in Parliament, and a provision designed to protect Catholic schools and to guarantee them a fair share of government funding.

Although there was still opposition to Confederation in Canada East, it cannot be assumed that the idea of union was brutally imposed on the population. Both profound causes and immediate motives led a good proportion of French Canadians to be in favour of it, the principal reason being that, rightly or wrongly, they feared annexation to the United States and viewed Confederation as the only way to prevent this.

Shortly after the conclusion of the Quebec Conference, the *Journal de Québec* seems to have represented a large part of public opinion when it wrote: "We want to be a nation one day and as that is our necessary destiny and the goal to which we aspire, we prefer the political condition of which we will be a vital element, and in which we will still be in existence, rather than to be thrown into the midst of an immense people like a drop of water lost in the ocean, where in a few years we would lose our language, our laws, and even the memory of our glorious origins."

The great artist who succeeded in channelling all the latent forces in French Canada was George-Étienne Cartier. Although he sometimes found himself in difficult circumstances, being at grips with a colleague as wily as John A. Macdonald, Cartier always sought concrete solutions. He did have, however, like many other politicians after him, a conception of federalism and the division of powers between the federal and provincial levels that was too simplified and optimistic.

While accepting federalism as inevitable, the French Canadians had only rudimentary ideas of what was involved or how it would work in practice. There was little recognition of the complications that would arise from the federal government having jurisdiction over immigration, cultural policy and health and welfare, for example.

As time went on, French Canadian members of Parliament had to consider, debate and legislate in these areas, where often their wishes for their Quebec constituents were in conflict with what Parliament wanted for Canadians as a whole. While members from other provinces experience the same kinds of conflicts, the problem is magnified for Quebec members who represent a constituency that has particularly strong cultural and historic differences from other Canadians.

In late 1866, a third intercolonial conference was held in London, England, and on Christmas Eve, the resolutions were translated into a Bill, which was put before the British Parliament. The Bill received third and final reading on March 19, 1867, and the *British North America Act* came into effect on July 1, 1867, bringing into being the new Dominion of Canada.

The central control proposed in the Quebec Resolutions was only partially reflected in the BNA Act. In 1892, Lord Watson of the Privy Council said of the Act, "The object of the Act was neither to weld the provinces into one, nor to subordinate provincial governments to a central authority, but to create a federal government in which they should all be represented, entrusted with the exclusive administration of affairs in which they had a common interest, each province retaining its independence and autonomy." In case after case this rationale was reflected in decisions favouring provincial independence and autonomy right up to 1949, when the Supreme Court of Canada replaced the Judicial Committee of the British Privy Council as the highest Court of Appeal for Canada.

While the United States of America came into being with Boston tea parties, shots that were heard around the world and a saucy thumbing of the nose at the monarch in England, and while the Republic of France was born by chopping off the heads of the reigning monarchs, a softer, gentler spirit presided at the birth of modern Canada. The new state came into being like the flutter of a dove's wing — in keeping with one aspect of Canadian character, the tendency to avoid drama and show.

A paradox exists, however, when one considers the scale of the Centennial celebrations. Unlike the two-hundredth anniversary celebrations marking Bastille Day in France, which were mostly fireworks extravaganzas, and unlike the two-hundredth anniversary of the *Declaration of Independence* in the United States, the marking of which was left to the private sector and ended up a fizzle, Canada's celebration stood foursquare on the theoretical underpinnings discussed in Chapter 1. There may not have been much fuss about our beginnings but in true Canadian fashion we were quiet and assured, thorough and acting in good taste when it came time to formally observe them.

To conclude our historical review, no sooner had the ink dried on the *British North America Act* than things started happening to bring the West into the Canadian fold. In the very year of Confederation, 1867, Russia sold Alaska to the United

States. This made the United States not only a Pacific power, but also a North Pacific power and a threat to the British-controlled Northwest Territories (now the Canadian western provinces).

The conclusion of the American Civil War in April 1865 released pent-up expansionist forces, and as more Americans moved west and north, a vigorous campaign started for the annexation of the Northwest. The new president, Ulysses S. Grant, was determined and outspoken in his desire to acquire Canada, and his secretary of state, Hamilton Fish, brought the matter up on several occasions in discussion with Britain's ambassador in Washington (Britain still having control of the Northwest at the time). Later, in the summer of 1867, Secretary of State W.H. Seward publicly affirmed his belief that Nature had intended that the whole continent should become one "within the magic circle of the American union."

The British government came to realize it would soon have to take action in these Northwest Territories, because part of this area was already occupied by thousands of miners, mostly Americans, who might set up a provisional government and demand union with the United States. Governor James Douglas of Vancouver Island came up with a partial solution to the problem by arbitrarily extending his authority to the mainland, thus anchoring at least the Pacific slope into a rapidly expanding Canada.

In 1868, the hot breath of American interests was felt once again in the Northwest when the Minnesota legislature demanded that the whole of the Northwest be annexed to the United States. The new Canadian Parliament sprang into action, citing Section 146 of the BNA Act, which provided for the admission of "Rupert's Land and the Northwest Territory" to the union on terms to be arranged.

After some nifty negotiations, the Hudson's Bay Company surrendered nearly all its leased land and the province of Manitoba was created with the passage of the *Manitoba Act* in 1870. These actions demonstrated to the United States and particularly to Minnesota that British and Canadian authority would be maintained in the Northwest. In 1871, British Columbia delegates to Ottawa negotiated extremely generous terms from the Dominion, including the pledge to begin the Pacific Railway within two years and to complete it within ten years of the date of union. On July 1, 1871, British Columbia became a full-fledged province with responsible government and control of its public lands. And little Prince Edward Island, having held out for "better terms," joined in 1873. In 1905, Saskatchewan and Alberta were created, together with the Yukon and Northwest Territories, where commissioners were appointed, self-government to come to those territories later.

Newfoundland, the easternmost 43,000-square-mile land mass of the North American continent, the island site of Viking ruins dating from 1000 AD, had been Britain's territory since 1497 and a colony since 1824. Because of its isolation it played little part in Confederation politics. The Maritimes were always understood to mean Nova Scotia, New Brunswick and Prince Edward Island but not Newfoundland. A delegate from Newfoundland was scheduled to attend the Quebec Conference as an observer but as he was on the point of embarking on the sea voyage to the mainland, his wife gave birth to a son, and he cancelled his plans in order to remain at her side. Serious Confederation talk did not take place until much later, when the Liberal firebrand Joey Smallwood, after several agonizing referenda, convinced Newfoundlanders to give up their British citizenship and become Canadians. The island province entered Confederation in 1949. Smallwood revelled in the 1967 celebrations, gleefully pronouncing that he was the only living Father of Confederation.

This brief and highly selective historical account reveals how the destiny of nations, like that of individuals, hangs on slender threads. The people of each western province and Newfoundland rejoiced as much as anyone in 1967, even though the majority of them had been but gleams in the eyes of the Fathers of Confederation one hundred years before.

In romantic literature, Confederation would be called the Birth of a Nation. In reality, it was not exactly a nation that was born. The year 1867 saw the birth of a modern political state, a new country of federal form, but within the new union, there was no sense of belonging to a unified nation. Quebeckers already considered themselves a nation. They had always been certain of their identity. The degree of certainty concerning national identity was less in other parts of Canada.

A Canadian identity was nevertheless in the making, and some of the variety inherent in that identity was revealed in the Confederation story itself.

We were brought together because we needed each other, we were good for each other — the basis of many a personal union.

Confederation was the work of an elite group of politicians, and this set a precedent. Canadians traditionally have trusted their leaders and conformed willingly to established policies.

The influence of the United States was a cardinal external factor forcing the "birth" of the new Canadian identity. We are North Americans all right, but not Americans, and that distinction helps establish our identity. American domination remains a threat, however, and the continuous cultural swamping and far too often bully-boy tactics coming from south of the border tend to render fuzzy the clear outlines of Canada's identity.

Central Canada, Ontario and Quebec, provided the push for Confederation — not the Atlantic provinces and certainly not the West, which was not even at the table. Today both the Maritimes and the West feel misunderstood and left out of the mainstream. Although the federal government tries to mollify their sense of alienation through various regional economic development programs and other devices, the feeling remains.

The Quebec Conference, held in English only, with no audible protest from the Francophone delegates, stands as a symbol of the subtle linguistic and cultural abuse that Anglophone Canadians have carried out against Francophones ever since. It is true that Prime Minister Trudeau made strong attempts to correct this situation, but his policies were only partially successful, and Canadian identity is still influenced by the bilingual boogeyman.

One identity-shaping factor that was not present in 1867 was ethnic diversity. The Chinese had not yet come to build the railroad. Ukrainians had not yet opened up the west. There were no Poles and Finns to mine ore in northern Ontario and there were no Japanese to fish or Sikhs to harvest timber on the west coast. Only a few blacks had come off the Underground Railroad in Halifax and Windsor.

In 1867 the main ethnic groups were English, Irish, Scottish and French and the widely scattered, mainly ghettoized aboriginals. Today, the situation is much different. According to Statistics Canada, over half the Canadian population now describe their ancestry as other than English, Irish, Scottish or French. And that ethnic mix was already coming together in Centennial year. In 1967 Canada celebrated an identity that had changed considerably since the country was first formed.

Reinforcement of identity is number one in *The Anniversary Axiomatique* for a reason. Because it is the most important. If Canada as a country could speak with one voice, it would say "I am... ." All components would be included: what it has accomplished, what it believes, what it possesses, what it hopes for. In the chapters to come, you will see how sometimes overtly, sometimes subtly, the "I am" components were reinforced in Canada in 1967.

CHAPTER *3*

Canada in the Sixties

A S THE CENTENNIAL ORGANIZERS were hunkering down to work in the early sixties, the Canadian-built satellite *Alouette* had been launched from Vandenberg Air Force Base, Marshall McLuhan had published *Understanding Media* and T.C. Douglas had been elected as first leader of the New Democratic Party at its founding convention in Ottawa. Like all Western nations after World War II, Canada was undergoing rapid social and economic change, and new issues were emerging that would reach the critical stage late in the decade, after Centennial was over. Of course, Canada did not choose to have its Centennial in the midst of a decade of change, but the social atmosphere of the times created excitement that added lustre and optimism to the hundredth-anniversary celebrations. It could be considered a benefit to be holding a unifying and identity-affirming party in the midst of upheaval. The greater degree of challenge presented holds promise of a greater degree of success.

Canada's Centennial organizers did not look at their country's socio-economic trends in detail but they might have benefited from such a pulse-taking. Because they failed to take into full account the changing atmosphere in Quebec, they were in no position to counteract the separatist trends emerging there.

Other phenomena — such as the burgeoning youth population — were more obvious, and the Centennial celebrations included events and programs to meet their needs. The organizers would certainly have been in a better position to macro-plan, however, if they had considered fully the socio-economic trends that will be described in this chapter. A lesson for organizers of future anniversary celebrations.

The sixties were the Diefenbaker and Pearson years — with the charismatic Trudeau making his first appearance in Parliament in 1965. It was a prosperous decade, as manufacturing increased substantially, mostly in the Quebec-Windsor corridor and largely as a result of the 1965 Canada-U.S. *Automotive Products Agreement*, which established free trade in automobiles and parts. In that same year, the gross national product had exceeded $50 billion a year, and the Organization for Economic Co-operation and Development had listed Canada as the second most affluent country in the world after the United States. Unfortunately, the wealth was concentrated in central Canada, and regions like the Maritimes continued to suffer from relatively low incomes. In 1965 the average annual family income in the Maritimes was less than the national average of $5,449 and the unemployment rate was twice as high as the national average. Regional inequity that had existed ever since Confederation.

The Far North and the Prairie provinces were also at a disadvantage, although John Diefenbaker attempted to rectify this situation. During his tenure as prime minister, he arranged for wheat sales to China and instituted agricultural reform that gave western farmers a boost. The "Northern Vision" that he preached during the 1957 and 1958 elections had less concrete results, but it did increase public awareness of the North and resulted in some economic development.

The overall economic boom created demand for labour and since there were not enough native-born Canadians around to fill the jobs, Ottawa finally relaxed immigration barriers to allow southern Europeans into the country in large numbers. In the 1960s, the government also began to chip away at the colour barrier, opening Canada's doors to West Indian, East Indian, Hong Kong and Mainland Chinese, Korean and Southeast Asian immigrants. The result was a changed face for Canada's largest cities — especially Toronto, which was transformed from a dull, British-dominated burg to a cosmopolitan centre. Between immigration and the baby boom that had been going on since the end of World War II, Canada's population grew by leaps and bounds. Between 1941 and 1951, the population went up by more than 20 percent, and between 1951 and 1961 it had zoomed up by 30 percent to more than 18 million.

Population pressure and corporate concentration changed the physical aspect of Canada's cities as well, as suburbs pushed the city limits into neighbouring farmers' fields, freeways began to circle cities, and downtown houses were razed to make way for high-rise apartments and office buildings. By 1961, 69.7 percent of Canadians lived and worked in urban areas. Place Ville-Marie in Montreal, the Toronto-Dominion Centre in Toronto and Elvedon House in Calgary were built — all towering but impersonal monuments to Canada's new prosperity. One of the more infamous developments occurred when Africville, a historic black community in Halifax, was bulldozed to make way for new development. Although the residents were relocated at government expense, they hated their new quarters, which became a symbol of thoughtless urban development.

As the decade wore on, more and more citizens became incensed at the way downtowns were being transformed, and ratepayers' groups were formed to protest what they perceived to be a loss of humane living environments. A *cause célèbre* in point: the successful opposition of the building of the Spadina Expressway — which would have cut through many stable Toronto neighbourhoods, spoiling the urbanscape, a heavy price to pay for "progress."

Protest and counter-culture were a dominant part of the sixties — mostly because of the baby boomers who were entering their teen years at the beginning of the decade. By 1963, the university student population was four times higher than in 1940 and many new universities had been created: Carleton University in 1957, York University in 1959, University of Waterloo in 1959, and University of Victoria and Trent University in 1963. The huge student population, liberated from old sexual mores by the invention and widespread marketing of the Pill and resentful of an older generation that had created the Bomb, launched protests against the established authorities. They succeeded in having some effect on curriculum and the extent to which the university ruled their private lives. The student movement became politicized as protests were made in support of the American civil rights movement and against U.S. involvement in the Vietnam war. And then there were the draft dodgers: thirty thousand of them by the end of the decade. With their baggage, some of them brought the politics of the New Left, which included elements of anarchism and heretical Marxism and attached itself to the hippie culture of relaxed morals, pacifism and political decentralization. The combination made Ottawa a bit nervous. Added to this was the accelerating widespread use of marijuana and LSD. A totally new phenomenon in Canada.

Attempting to respond to the situation, and as a means of providing young people with employment, Ottawa set up the Company of Young Canadians (CYC) in 1966. The objective was to train young Canadians to work on community programs, helping society's underdogs to improve their lives. From the government's point of view, however, the program backfired. Many members of the CYC operated according to separatist and Marxist principles, embarrassing the government and provoking it to impose controls that were unacceptable to the CYCers, causing bitterness and misunderstanding.

Shifts in values were also significant on the religious scene. Established churches were losing credibility and attendance as faith in science and "observed reality" increased. Reflecting the mood of the times, Pierre Berton's *Comfortable Pew* charged that churches were out of touch with current issues. In the face of these accusations, some churches began to pay more attention to social problems, but some adhered even more strictly to orthodox views. In his encyclical *Mater et Magistra*, issued in 1961, Pope John XXIII responded to the issue by calling the Roman Catholic Church to become less complacent and more involved in society.

Though still searching for its spiritual and political identity, Canada was proud of its position in the world at the beginning of the sixties. During the Suez Crisis of 1956, Lester B. Pearson, then secretary of state for external affairs, had established Canada's reputation as a peacemaker, and the country continued to take this role seriously. In July 1960, Canada sent peacekeeping troops to the Congo, and when the UN intervened in the conflict between Greeks and Turks on Cyprus in 1964, Secretary of State for External Affairs Paul Martin played an important part in setting up the Cyprus UN peacekeeping force.

Canada's position in the world may have been well defined, but on the home front, its identity was not so clear. Since Confederation, Canada has defined itself as a separate entity on a continent dominated by the United States. But a question always recurs: How separate should we be?

There are good reasons for close association with the United States. In the 1950s, for instance, when the threat of a nuclear strike from the U.S.S.R. was felt to be real, Canada entered into the *North American Air Defence Agreement* (NORAD) with the United States, which allowed for the integration of Canadian and U.S. air-defence forces. A mutually beneficial situation, but not without its hazards. When Diefenbaker's government announced in 1957 that two squadrons of the American anti-aircraft missile *Bomarc* would be brought onto Canadian soil, no one objected. But when it became known that the missiles were to be fitted with nuclear warheads, Diefenbaker changed his mind, and relations with the United States soured. Then in 1963 Pearson reversed the decision and the warheads were delivered to Canada. The whole thing was a bungle — and evidence of how difficult it is for a small country like Canada to define its identity and desires, living next door to a superpower like the United States.

Canada's attempts to define its economic independence from the United States were no more consistent. In 1965, a *Maclean's* magazine poll showed that Canadians were open to the concepts of foreign investment and free trade with the United States. But by Centennial year, the responses to a *Toronto Daily Star* poll were much more nationalistic: 67 percent thought that the Canadian government should take steps to reduce foreign control of Canadian industry and 63 percent believed that Canada did not demonstrate enough independence in dealing with the United States. In the same year, George P. Grant published his famous *Lament for a Nation*, which drew a bleak picture of Canada being integrated into the United States and a new tyrannical state emerging as a result.

Pearson's Liberal government did nothing to discourage a close economic association with the United States — in spite of the nationalist economic proposals of his minister of finance, Walter Gordon. This apparent passivity led members of the English Canadian public to set up nationalist organizations by the end of the decade. It is impossible to know whether the Centennial festivities and Expo had anything to do with galvanizing this nationalist feeling, but like so many other trends, this one culminated shortly after the country's one-hundredth anniversary when a number of nationalist organizations were set up.

On the literary and cultural scene, a Canadian voice was beginning to develop by the early sixties, but it, too, was threatened by American dominance. The 1951 *Report of the Massey Royal Commission on National Development in the Arts, Letters and Sciences* had warned of this phenomenon, and as a result of its recommendations, the National Library had been set up in 1953 and the Canada Council in 1957. These agencies were not enough to ensure Canadian control of its own culture (the battle with the elephant to the south is an ongoing one), but they set the stage for a decade in which Canadian literature and arts began to come into their own. Instrumental in the fostering of interest in Can Lit was Jack McClelland, who became president of McClelland and Stewart in 1961. He published classic works in Canadian literature, brought out the first two volumes of the *Canadian Centenary Series* in 1963 and became one of the most important catalysts in the publication of original works of Canadian fiction.

Meanwhile, CBC-TV was offering Canadians images of themselves in public affairs shows like "Point de mire" (1956-59) hosted by René Lévesque, "Front Page Challenge" and "This Hour Has Seven Days." The government-funded station also provided all-Canadian entertainment in the form of the "Tommy Hunter Show," Wayne and Shuster specials and telecasts of National Hockey League games. Was the literary and broadcasting community successful in solidifying Canadian identity? More or less. But American sit-coms and public affairs shows kept streaming through, with no respect of boundaries — an inevitable and not entirely regrettable state of affairs, but one that did not necessarily give Canadians a more sophisticated sense of identity.

There was one area in which Canadians did successfully beg to differ from their friends south of the forty-ninth parallel, and that was in social services. Although Canada went through the same kind of free-enterprise industrial development as the United States after World War II, it soon began to show social interventionist tendencies that were foreign to the American way. In Quebec, private electrical companies were nationalized to form Hydro-Québec (an idea suggested by René Lésvesque in 1962), and in Saskatchewan, medicare had been introduced early in the decade.

At the national level, medicare was introduced in 1957 and extended to cover doctors' services in 1966. The Canada Pension Plan came into effect in 1966 and in the same year, the Guaranteed Income Supplement program was established to provide a supplement to pensioners with little or no income beyond their old-age-security pension. Canada was now a welfare state — a humane, if heavily taxed, society.

The biggest identity question that we Centennial planners should have been asking ourselves related to Quebec and its place in Confederation. Since World War II, Quebec had undergone the same industrialization and urbanization as the rest of Canada, but the governing Union Nationale party still operated out of a paternalistic, conservative ideology and the Roman Catholic Church had responsibility for education, hospitals and assistance to the poor. This situation turned around abruptly after Jean Lesage led the Liberals to victory in the 1960 election.

The Lesage government's philosophy, *maîtres chez nous* (masters in our own house), encouraged Quebeckers to ignore Ottawa (and Canada) as much as possible and to think of themselves as a French Canadian state. Acting on this philosophy, the Liberals launched the "Quiet Revolution" — a set of sweeping reforms in education, social security and labour regulation. A commission of inquiry into education recommended the creation of a Department of Education (thus shifting control of schools away from the Roman Catholic Church and over to the government). The Caisse de Dépôt et Placement du Québec was created in 1965 to control the assets of the Quebec Pension Plan, and Hydro-Québec was formed. Both of these developments were sources of great national pride for Quebeckers. But when Quebec went so far as to sign cultural and educational agreements with France, the federal government stepped in and pointed out that there could be only one representative to foreign countries — Ottawa.

Rudely awakened to the fact of a disgruntled Quebec, Pearson's government was quick to respond with a policy of "co-operative federalism," and the Bilingualism and Biculturalism Commission was sent across Canada to investigate how Quebec could be accommodated within Confederation.

The forces of discontent were too strong to contain, however, and separatism, which can be traced in Quebec to as early as 1905, began to gain momentum. The most significant separatist group of the time was the Rassemblement pour l'indépendance nationale (RIN), which won over 9 percent of the vote in the 1966 Quebec election. Violent agitators and terrorists were also on the scene, however, including the Fédération de Libération du Québec (FLQ), which was founded in March 1963 to use propaganda and terrorism to promote the emergence of an independent socialist Quebec. In 1963 they set off bombs in mailboxes in Montreal and three federal armouries. In 1964 they stole $50,000 in cash and military equipment and held up International Firearms and killed a vice-president. Pierre Vallières wrote a book describing Québécois as *Nègres blancs d'Amérique*. Inflammatory stuff. Within a decade the FLQ would cause a kidnapping, an execution, the invoking of the *War Measures Act* and suspension of civil liberties.

It is said that the actions of radicals tend to soften up the middle ground. It happened in Quebec. In the election of 1970 a separtist goverment came into power in the province.

Incredibly, Canadians outside Quebec seemed to have little awareness that the effects of the Quiet Revolution meant greater demands on the rest of Canada. Few members of the general public realized the extent of Quebec's disenchantment and how indifferent Quebeckers were to the upcoming Centennial celebrations. Misperceptions and ignorance for which all of Canada was to pay.

Two other important minority groups began to raise their voices in the sixties: native people and women. In 1963 the native infant mortality rate was 97 per 1,000 (four times the national average), and in 1965, a federal-provincial conference on poverty and opportunity condemned the Third World living conditions on most reserves. Native politicial organization was still embryonic at best, but the beginnings were there: in 1961 the National Indian Council was established, and William Wutunee, a Cree lawyer living in Calgary, warned that native peoples across Canada had to get to know each other so they could present a more common political front. Wutunee and other native leaders were part of a trend that culminated after Centennial in the 1969 appearance of Harold Cardinal's *The Unjust Society*, which revealed the injustices to natives living in the "Just Society" that Prime Minister Pierre Trudeau had promised to establish.

On the cultural front, native Canadians were beginning to make their voices heard more clearly, and to capture the imaginations of non-natives. In 1962, the Ojibwa artist Norval Morrisseau exhibited paintings at a Toronto art gallery and sold out on opening night. Inuit carvings and prints had been sold in the south since the late forties, but this commerce increased after Inuit co-operatives were established, beginning in the late fifties.

By the early sixties, Canadian women were also becoming more aware of inequities that made them second-class citizens in a supposedly equitable society. Feminists had been aware of these injustices for decades, but as the Pill now allowed women to control their fertility, they had more freedom to work outside the home and establish careers, a phenomenon that brought women's issues into the public forum. Questions of equal pay and equal rights to property within marriage began to be debated, and in 1964, the Quebec government raised the legal status of married women to that of a major. (Previously, they were considered minors.) Political action groups were not yet a significant force, however. Although an anti-nuke demonstration was organized on Parliament Hill by the Voice of Women in 1961, most political action groups were not formed until after Centennial year. It was 1971 before the National Action Committee on the Status of Women was formed as an umbrella organization for women's groups.

As 1967 approached, Canada was suffering from growing pains and identity crises in most areas of its collective life. Fortunately, however, the overall mood in the sixties was one of optimism, and it was with great hopes for its future that Canada headed into Centennial year.

CHAPTER 4

Beginnings and Getting Organized

N<small>O PRESCRIPTION CAN BE GIVEN</small> for the way an anniversary organizing group should be set up. In the case of national celebrations, however, the anniversary impulse will inevitably arise from non-government as well as government sources — although in most cases the organizing body will be government-controlled.

Advance planning is also a tremendous asset, of course, but as we shall see, Canada stumbled in this area — as well as in the choice of certain personnel. The Canadian model, though it evolved at a snail's pace at first, was a success in the end because it combined openness to ideas from the public with eventual clear direction from a single government-appointed agency. For all its gropings in the dark, if the government had taken a more *laissez-faire* approach to the celebrations and allowed the private sector to handle everything, the Centennial year celebrations would definitely have been less coherent and unifying. Although numerous private sector entities were hired to prepare for the grand event, all policies and procedures were set by the Centennial Commission — and the Commission itself received the attention of a high-level member of government who would ultimately be held accountable for the success of the celebrations.

Canada got off to a slow start for the same reason that any government would drag its heels in preparing for celebrations. Governments of any stripe are reluctant to spend money on programs where there will be no evident payoff during their term of office. If the results will not appear for ten years, governments reason that they will do them no good. Long-term projects may be good public policy, but they are bad politics.

In the late 1950s this phenomenon was at work. The federal administration at the time — Diefenbaker's Tories — had no strong motivation to set up a structure for a celebration that would take place when they might no longer be in office. And anyway, who knew what ephemera might be generated and how one might quantify the benefit to the populace?

There was a third factor: simple procrastination. 1967 was such a long way off. Politicians no doubt felt that there was no point even thinking about the celebrations until they were closer. If they were still in office when the Centennial was being celebrated, they might benefit. If they were not, it would be someone else's problem and there would be no point making plans for a celebration that would only add to the glory of another government.

The anniversary compulsion was not to be stopped, however, and since no impetus was forthcoming from government, the private sector stepped in to fill the breach. In spite of Canada's traditional habit of letting the government do what it wants, the anniversary compulsion overcame certain members of the populace — and they filled the vacuum. And vacuum there was, for like any government, the Canadian Parliament was generally cautious, often uncertain, slow to sense a public need and dilettante in forming a response.

On the other hand, non-government organizations (NGOs) can be bold, vociferous, very sensitive to public need and quite articulate in exposing this need. And they have nothing to lose politically. Witness the function performed by such organizations as Pollution Probe, Greenpeace and Amnesty International. Each of these groups sensitizes governments to a need, lead governments into action and help establish standards that later became Legislative norms.

So it was with the Centennial of Confederation in Canada. The YMCA, the YWCA, the Canadian Conference of Christians and Jews, the Canadian Citizenship Council and the Canadian Amateur Sports Federation were typical of organizations that started writing to the federal government urging some kind of action. Some, like the Citizenship Council, had pure citizen-building motives in mind. Others, like the Canadian Conference of Christians and Jews, had student exchange programs underway and saw that if these could be enlarged in scope, *this* aspect of citizenship could be aggrandized. One, the Royal Architectural Institute of Canada, probably foresaw Centennial monuments in the offing and agitated for action, realizing it takes time to design and build monuments.

The executive director of this last organization, Robbins Elliott, was most vociferous, as was the executive director of the Canadian Citizenship Council, Alan Clark. These two, with Dr. Roby Kidd and others, starting in 1959-60, led what became a mini-movement, which eventually and officially became the Canadian Centenary Council (CCC). At the time a formal group existed called the Association of Association Executives. These were the Elliotts and Clarks of the NGO world. They had much in common and often worked in concert to bring pressure on governments. Their individual constituencies, taken in aggregate, formed a sizeable body representing as they did the vast array of plural elements found in a modern society. Here was the ready-made membership for the new Canadian Centenary Council.

They communicated in writing with the prime minister's office, the secretary of state (the office in Canada generally responsible for cultural matters), and other departments, and by letters to the editors of papers read by politicians and officials. Such letters in some cases were attributed to the president of the CCC, and many others were attributed to leaders such as Clark and Elliott. A compound lobby was created.

The Canadian Centenary Council consisted of more than a score of organizations and a board representing all regions of

Canada, and it was chaired by Dr. Norman A. MacKenzie, president of the University of British Columbia. Their stated purpose was to promote the idea of celebrations commemorating the events of 1864 and 1867. They held several well-publicized meetings in various cities of Canada, including Ottawa, the members paying their own way (and in Canada that is a significant matter if one lives in Vancouver and the meeting is in Halifax). Among the themes of these meetings were "Biculturalism: The Basis of Canadian Society" (here was early recognition in the anniversary context of the dual nature of Canada) and "Awareness Canada" in 1963 and "Centennial Planning Canada-Wide" and "World's Fair" in 1964. The Council also conducted "blitz sessions" across the country, in which teams of planning experts gave assistance to corporate and voluntary organizations that had not yet made definite Centennial plans.

The representatives of not-for-profit organizations who attended the meetings were financed by their associations but it soon became apparent that they could not attend often. Nor could their organizations be expected to finance and coordinate events, programs and projects on a national scale.

The members of the Council were non-government people, so some of them were from the world of commerce. They hoped that Canada's great corporate commercial entities would develop a Centennial program, or at least projects, given that they had the resources to do so. Many attempts were made to gain the support of large corporations, some quite vigorous. Others were unprofessionally feeble, and except for one or two rare exceptions, nothing happened. One notable exception was the Royal Bank of Canada which, in 1967, made an unconditional gift of $50,000 to a Canadian of merit, and pledged to repeat this generosity each succeeding year, indefinitely.

It gradually became clear that the public relations advisors in the business offices across the country felt their firms would get more mileage and visibility from supporting Expo '67, the World's Fair that was to be held in Montreal during the Centennial year.

Many ideas developed by members of the Council were later adopted. Among them were plans for a Centennial symbol; for an exhibit of Canada's past and present, later translated into travelling trains and caravans; and the establishment of a system of travel subsidies to encourage Canadian youths to visit other regions of Canada. As these ideas percolated, official Ottawa was listening in. Then, late in the spring of 1961, in the middle of the Diefenbaker administration, officials in the Privy Council Office, the bureaucratic unit that serves the Cabinet in its decision-making function, were instructed to prepare a memorandum to Cabinet outlining how the government should deal with the impending Centennial.

One of the results was that by 1962 the Privy Council Office had designed a National Conference on the Centennial of Confederation, a virtual clone of the Canadian Centenary Council, even to the point of naming to this Conference many members of the Council who thus served on both bodies. The Conference's function was identical to that of the Council but it had one huge advantage — the capacity to throw the whole weight of the federal-provincial government apparatus behind the Centennial.

The Canadian government spent a long time getting over its inertia but, once it got moving, it completely eclipsed the efforts of the voluntary agency sector.

The Council had another vestigial influence in that many of its constituent members had time to refine their ideas concerning Centennial programs and projects and were well positioned to importune key people within the government and the National Conference as their functions began to clarify. Council members now actively lobbied senior staff with precise proposals for programs and projects. At the time, they knew more about what to do than staff, and since the Council did not have any programs or projects of its own, it was natural for its members to seek funding for their ideas from senior staff.

Eventually, without a *raison d'être*, the Canadian Centenary Council became weak, atrophied and died although it did not officially end its days until March 13, 1967. Along the way the executive director, Norbert Prefontaine was absorbed into the staff of the Centennial Commission and the chairman was appointed to its board, but not to the Executive Committee.

The very existence of the Canadian Centenary Council was evidence of a striving for citizen participation. Through this body, a number of dedicated individuals and organizations succeeded in influencing the shape of the first Centennial projects and, more important, they made the public and the government aware of the significance of the impending Centennial.

It would be wrong to say, however, that the Canadian Centenary Council embodied a grassroots enthusiasm for the celebration to come. In fact, its history reveals dramatically how Canadians are willing to "leave it to government," and how they are passive about the resulting process. Once the programs are in place, they become enthusiastic in their compliance with what is to be done, and obedient in their participation as directed. That's part of the Canadian way.

Yes, official Ottawa had been listening. The first high-level official to become involved in the Centennial plans was Robert Bryce, secretary to the Cabinet and clerk of the Privy Council, the most senior career officer in the whole Public Service of Canada. The senior of seniors. In Britain, secretaries to the Cabinet have been called Knights in Office, Lords thereafter. In Canada they eventually get gonged as C.C., Companions of the Order of Canada. They preside over the Privy Council Office (PCO), sometimes called the Cabinet Office. The most sensitive, powerful section of the government's central decision-making apparatus.

The PCO is staffed by a small elite group of professional public sector personnel. Positions are *never* advertised. One is asked to join the PCO. The best and the brightest are drawn into this talent pool. A stint in the PCO is *de rigueur* if one aspires to deputy minister rank.

In the early sixties the Privy Council Office resided in the Nepean sandstone 1864 Gothic pile known as the East Block. That is where the Cabinet met, in the ornate blue and gold Victorian room with its oval table and red leather chairs. There it was in early 1961 that Robert Bryce called into his second-floor office Dr. John Hodgson, Ph.D., O.B.E., an economist with a distinguished career in the Canadian Navy. He had been drawn to the PCO from a senior executive post at the Central Mortgage and Housing Corporation.

"John," Bryce trumpeted, "we'd better do something about this Centennial business. Look into it and let me know what you think."

No time limit. No parameters.

Dr. Hodgson represented the best type of Privy Council officer. Well-rounded academically, seasoned as an executive officer in the Navy, experienced as a manager and administrator, disciplined, thoroughly professional. And he played beautiful classical piano for relaxation. Starting with only an abstract concept, the Centennial of Confederation in Canada, he proceeded to design a structure and process to give it life. A draft memorandum to Cabinet was prepared, setting out the problem, the pros and cons of various solutions, then conclusions and recommendations.

Following staff discussion, the draft became a formal memorandum to Cabinet, and after liaison work with the Department of Justice and the House leader in the House of Commons, a bill was drafted to be put before Parliament. After due procedure this became Chapter 60 of the *Revised Statutes of Canada 9.10 Elizabeth II, An Act Respecting the Observance of the Centennial of Confederation in Canada*. It received Royal Assent and was proclaimed as law on September 29, 1961. Clause 3 of the Act stated, "There shall be a corporation to be called the National Centennial Administration" (two years later its name would be changed to "Centennial Commission").

John Hodgson's next task was to find acceptable individuals to form the corpus, and normally he would have turned to the minister responsible for the Administration as well as to a colleague in the PCO who maintained a list of eligible, desirable (and sometimes needy) parties, who are available to fill the over one thousand governor-in-council appointments that have to be filled each year.

But an unusual set of circumstances prevailed. The Right Honourable John George Diefenbaker had just been through an election and was returned to power as Canada's prime minister all right, but while his party, the Progressive Conservatives, had garnered more seats than any one of the other parties, the aggregate seats of the others exceeded the number of Conservative seats. A minority government. A worrisome and distracting situation. Further, the Act established that the prime minister would be the minister responsible or "such other members of the Queen's Privy Council for Canada as is designated by the Governor-in-Council."

Mr. Diefenbaker remained responsible and never did appoint another. It is well established that Diefenbaker was a notorious procrastinator when it came to making appointments. He just couldn't make up his mind. So the Act remained a dead letter for over a year.

Finally, someone persuaded him to choose a head for the National Centennial Administration. It was a natural place to start, and clearly it was the most important of the appointments he would make.

Shift to Toronto. The office of the Canadian Tourist Association. The office of the executive director, John Wiggans Fisher.

John Fisher had made a national reputation for himself between 1943 and 1955 with "John Fisher Reports," the live radio show he broadcast nationally three times a week on CBC. His scripts he called "Pride Builders." His fans from coast-to-coast called him "Mr. Canada."

The phone rings.

"It's the prime minister's office calling," his secretary says.

"Hello."

"Mr. Fisher, the prime minister would like to see you tomorrow afternoon on the private car at track six at Union Station [Toronto's main railway station]. Can you make it?"

There's only one answer to that question. Yesterday, today and forever. John recalled making his way along the gritty sidewalk of the joint CN-CP rail yard west of Union Station to the mahogany-and-velour-lined 1936 vintage railway coach to keep this unexpected and mysterious appointment. The white-coated steward served coffee from the Tiffany sterling silver service and some small talk ensued. Then, "John, I want you to head up the Centennial Administration. You will be commissioner, and chairman of the board."

"Well, that's very flattering, but I am happy with what I'm doing and it sounds like a pretty big job."

"Would you like it if I put you in the Senate and you could run it from there?"

Mr. Canada knew that a general election was probably impending. He knew that to those fortunate enough to be incumbents in the Senate, the sweetest three words in the world the day after a general election, no matter what the result, are, "Good morning, Senator." For life.

Again there was only one answer to the proffered question. Yesterday, today and forever. It was the vision of the Red Chamber that propelled Mr. Canada into the biggest Pride Builder of his career.

But, alas, the election came too soon, and the Great Procrastinator never got around to fulfilling his promise. He lost the election of 1963, and with it his power melted away like butter in the sun, including the prerogative of appointing Canadians to the Senate.

Mr. Canada's glimpse of the prize was fleeting. Never to be seen again. He was destined to run things under two separate Liberal ministers, both of whom would prove to be far less compatible than Dief the Chief, who had appointed him. And he had no promise of security past 1967. Not even for one day and certainly not for life.

Fisher was appointed an executive assistant to Diefenbaker while he was waiting for the order-in-council to be passed appointing him chairman, and more important, senator. He wrote speeches for Diefenbaker, but was frustrated in this because Diefenbaker didn't read what he wrote. He just wanted something to hold in his hand. Then he made up his own speech. Fisher observed one time, "You could have pasted the funny papers on sheets of 8 x 10 and handed them to him with a glossy cover and he would say, 'Great, Great. Now here's what I'm going to say.'"

But Fisher's real work started with his official appointment in January 1963. Now he was a public servant. Now he was Commissioner, the head of the Commission, but so far the Commission itself was non-existent.

A commission is a corporate entity, the corpus or body being made up of a board of directors. There are two kinds of boards: leading boards and following boards. The practice of the former is for the general membership of the organization to appoint members and let them take the lead in choosing their chief executive officer. This is the strong, healthy approach. The practice of the latter is generally to allow the chief executive officer to make appointments — and it is possible that the CEO may choose people in his or her own image, a captive group. In either case the board members should represent the interests of the shareholders, and have a clear commitment to the objectives of the corporation.

In business, where the objective is to provide a good or service at a profit, the interest of the shareholders is clear. Profitability. In voluntary associations, the objective is to provide an optimum level of service to a constituency.

In government entities, where the constituents to be served may be a large segment of the population or perhaps the whole population, governments cannot take a chance on permitting a following board to develop. A hybrid is permissible but in any case the selection of the chief executive is absolutely crucial.

The type of board and CEO that are appropriate really depend on the task. Chrysler chairman and CEO Lee Iacocca was persuaded by a leading board to head the 1986 celebrations marking the one-hundredth anniversary of the installation of the Statue of Liberty, and with excellent results. He had the right stuff. This appears to be the desired model for anniversaries of this type.

In Canada, as far as governments are concerned, the pattern is for the executive branch of the government (the Cabinet) to select and appoint the chief executive officer first and let him or her choose a board (a following board). The governor of the Bank of Canada, for example, is appointed by Cabinet and then recommends who will be members of the board. Fisher's appointment followed this model.

John Wiggans Fisher was born and raised in Sackville, New Brunswick, and attended law school at Dalhousie University, receiving the degree Bachelor of Laws in 1937. The "Wiggans" part of his name came from his maternal grandfather, who was an Anglican minister and rector of the parish of Sackville for forty-eight years. A memorial to him reads: "A man of many interests and many friends, he was most beloved in the community, a true pastor to his people, a delightful companion, full of wit. He retained the agility and buoyancy of spirit of a young man... ." He died at age 92 in 1936, one year before Fisher received his law degree. This sentiment could have been applied to John. Indeed, in 1966 I visited his mother, the pastor's daughter, at the family home in Frosty Hollow, New Brunswick, to see if I could discover what made him tick. She told me that John had greatly admired his grandfather Wiggans and attempted to emulate him. But, she added, "John is still a little boy, he has never grown up."

Judy LaMarsh's assessment appears in her 1969 book, *Memoirs of a Bird in a Gilded Cage.* "An untidy looking man, he is warm, friendly and outgoing. He suffers from a lifetime of over-patted ego and a fear of the future." Pretty shrewd observation in light of his mother's comment.

He had a broad forehead that some would call "an intelligent forehead," a rather bulbous nose, fleshy sensuous lips, and mirthful eyes. He was flat-footed, and when he walked, his size-twelve shoes tracked straight ahead, splaying neither in nor out.

John was thought by his English-speaking public to be bilingual. He had taken a summer course at language school in Saint-Pierre and Miquelon but all he had retained were a few polite phrases. Because he had a mellifluous voice the phrases he did have evoked promise of much more to come. The

French greetings that opened his speeches provoked applause from the good ladies in Sillery, Quebec, who had determined at birth never to learn French, and approving glances in Meaford, Ontario. He never addressed a meeting of Québécois in French. He could not do it. And yet the myth persisted in Anglo territory that he was bilingual.

He had, during the Centennial year, an unfortunate and unhappy home life. His wife had been raped in her motel room while on a trip with John. She never recovered, was afraid to leave the house and lived as a recluse. Thus there was no real Mrs. Canada to share in the public acclaim. John, like countless before and since, accepted comfort from wherever it might come, and he had a vast female following on both coasts and all the way in between. Some were elegant and socially prominent. Some garden variety. All were devoted — and with reason. John at his most affable was a companion *sans pareil.*

He liked the grape but his consumption was not inordinate and it didn't interfere with his public appearances. He was not given to profanity and his rhetoric was consistently that of a gentleman. Except when he was provoked. Then it was thunder and lightning time. Thor incarnate.

Fisher was a lone wolf, a one-man band. He was very good at making speeches. He was not a good executive or manager or administrator. His principal value to the enterprise was his enthusiasm about the romantic ideal of Canada and his lyricism in describing various colourful Canadians and some Canadian historical events.

He should never have been put in charge of an organization the size of the Centennial Commission. What was needed was a superb proven executive. If Fisher could have been attached to such a person as a kind of roaming goodwill Centennial ambassador, that would have made sense.

The process that Diefenbaker should have started over a year before was reactivated in January 1963 and Privy Council officers helped John get organized. He was given great latitude in selecting his eight directors (later to be expanded to eleven), but no latitude in the appointment of deputy commissioner.

The Cabinet insisted on active participation in this appointment, and it was clearly indicated that a Francophone Québécois would have to be assigned to the post.

The reality of Canada's dual nature made this necessary. The difficulty was as follows: it would have been impossible to have co-equal French- and English-speaking leaders; one would inevitably dominate the other. It is also a difficult, if not impossible, task for a preselected board to choose two leaders and hope they will be compatible.

It appears that it was The Honourable Pierre Sévigny, associate minister of national defence, who came up with a respectable candidate — Robert Choquette, called the "Prince of Poets" by the Société de Poètes Canadiens Français. It was natural for Diefenbaker to look to one of his Cabinet in Quebec for a recommendation, but it was a hit-and-miss process. Sévigny summered at the resort area of Murray Bay, east of Quebec, a cliquish ghetto for upscale Montreal and Quebec City families — and so did Choquette. And it was here that he was approached and where he accepted this, yet another jewel in his already sparkling crown. Deputy commissioner of the Centennial Administration.

If there was ever a man of letters in Quebec, it was Robert Choquette. At the age of twenty-one he won the first of his three Prix Davids, for his poetry collection *A travers les vents*. His early radio series, "Le Curé de Village" and "La Pension Velder" were household "must hears." His epic poem "Suite Marine" won him the Prix International des Amitiés Françaises in 1954.

He was unknown in English-speaking Canada. A solid assumption would be that Diefenbaker had never heard of him. But it looked good, and because of his radio background, it might be thought that he and Fisher would have a lot in common. They might make a good team. And he might be just the man to stir up Centennial interest in Quebec.

It turned out, however, that he had been tragically miscast. The absolute epitome of gentleness, civility and sensitivity, with a delicious sense of humour, he would sit bolt upright at an empty desk in the big office provided for him in Ottawa and sign anything that was put in front of him without reading it. He did not appear to have a clue about what was going on or what was expected of him. The Prince of Poets had been parachuted into the wrong kingdom. He lasted less than a year.

Choquette was an absolutely delightful man: a gentle man and a gentleman, a prince indeed. But his contribution to the celebration of the Centennial of Confederation was, unfortunately, absolutely totally nil.

With the government bent on having Fisher head up the whole Centennial celebration, what they should have provided was a seasoned professional — someone who had proven ability in organization and management at a senior level. If you are going to appoint a figurehead to stand in the limelight, you'd better have a substantial powerhouse behind him to effectively propel the vessel. You certainly don't need two figureheads.

Georges Gauthier succeeded him (he had been head of the Pay Research Bureau, a semi-autonomous component of the Treasury Board). Gauthier had come to Ottawa to work for the Department of National Revenue and had painfully acquired English during his career in that department. He was the most "pure" Francophone in the whole place; he was very wise and cautious, and an excellent administrator. During Fisher's lengthy absences from Ottawa, he functioned as chairman of the Commission's board of directors and was the *de facto* chief executive and chief operating officer during the build-up to the Centennial celebrations. Whereas the original Act had called for a deputy commissioner, when it was revised in 1963, the position was moved up a notch to that of associate commissioner. Better conceptually and better in practice.

Gauthier accepted the difficult post on condition that he would have it in writing that he would be appointed deputy head of the Public Service Staff Relations Board after Centennial was over.

The organization chart on pages 56 and 57 will help you understand how the Centennial Commission was organized, and how the various parties related to each other and to other government entities. Working from the top down, it all starts with the minister, who during the Centennial preparations was first The Honourable Maurice Lamontagne and later The Honourable Judy LaMarsh. The "Honourable" part of the title denotes that each is a member of the Cabinet, which is the top executive group chosen by the prime minister from among elected members of Parliament of his own political party. The minister of public works, for example, directs what goes on in the Department of Public Works. The chief honchos in some departments are characterized differently: in the Department of External Affairs, the minister is called the Secretary of State for External Affairs, but still referred to as "the minister"; the boss at the Treasury Board is formally known as the President of the Treasury Board, but like all the others is "the minister"; Lamontagne and LaMarsh's official title was "Secretary of State" but each was also known as "the minister."

You will see the Treasury Board off to the side there. This committee of the Cabinet, made up of a very large staff, is the general manager of the whole government. It sets all kinds of management policies, controls the total budget and approves departmental budgets. This is the place where the Big Operational Picture is always kept in view.

Off to the same side is the Privy Council Office, or Cabinet Office, the PCO. The staff group headed by the secretary to the Cabinet serves the whole Cabinet and assists them as they deliberate and decide, and finally disseminates their decisions to the whole government system. On the chart the PCO appears shadowy because they work in the shadows.

In Canada the Department of the Secretary of State looks after cultural affairs and the dignified aspects of government. The Canadian Broadcasting Corporation, for instance, reports to Parliament through the secretary of state. It was the minister of this department, the secretary of state, who was at the top of the Centennial heap. The Centennial Commission reported to her. The Commission had statutory authority to do its job and was responsible to see that things happened, but the minister was ultimately accountable to the government for the performance

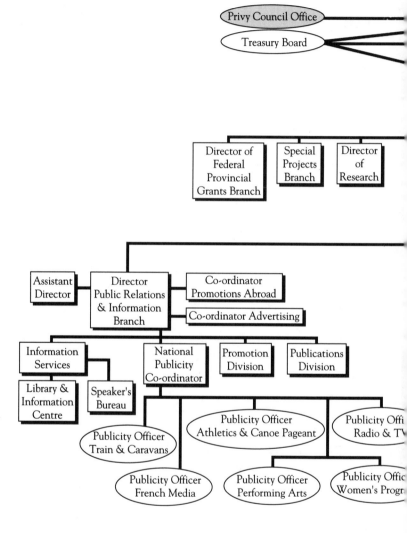

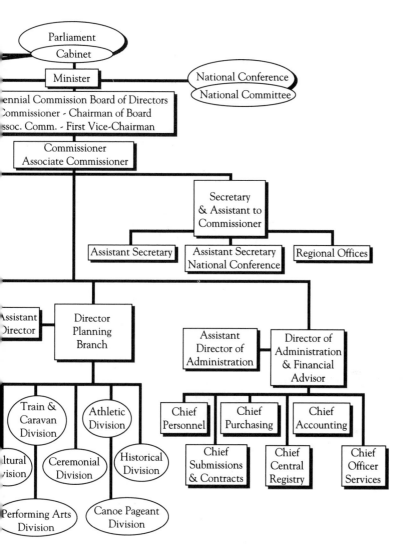

of the Commission and all its parts. Of course, ministers cannot look after the day-to-day operations of all aspects of their departments; that's the work of the armies of public servants hired to do the job, and the minister delegates supervision of that work to a deputy minister. (In the case of the secretary of state, the deputy minister is called the Undersecretary of State. Judy LaMarsh's undersecretary was Ernie Steele, who at one time had been secretary of the Treasury Board, another office having the rank of deputy minister).

John Fisher, commissioner of the Centennial Commission and chairman of its board of directors, also had the rank of deputy minister, and the Commission reported to the minister (and the government) through him. A typical structure is a broadly representative board of directors, with a smaller group chosen from among them as an Executive Committee which spends significant time considering details of the operation, both groups headed by the same person who is the chairperson — in this case, Fisher and his associate commissioner, Georges Gauthier. The latter would be present but not *preside*, doing so only in Fisher's absence.

The members of the board of directors were called "directors." They can be thought of as "outside" directors, unpaid and part-time. (They are on the organizational chart, neatly arranged, ready to give policy guidance and approve major expenditures.) But to do the work, they need senior line officers (the branch directors or inside directors), subordinate officers (the chiefs of divisions), and platoons of foot soldiers (the rest of the staff). The board needed one senior staff officer to look after its particular requirements when deliberating as a committee, and who in this case co-ordinated the work of regional offices. This was the secretary and assistant to the commissioners. Other people performed other specialized functions, but these positions formed the basic structure.

On the free advice side, the minister had the National Conference with the very effective National Committee at its heart, which performed a co-ordinating function. There they are, off to the right.

Each province had its own Centennial organization to absorb and modulate the Centennial programs and dollars flowing from the centre, the Centennial Commission in Ottawa. These are not shown on the chart.

The chart has some blobs rather than all neat little boxes because in reality an organization is rarely neat. Like the human body. No neat little square boxes. All blobs. But when it's in good health, it functions perfectly.

The composition of Fisher's board of directors was constrained by Canada's regional diversity and the need for all regions to be represented. There had to be someone from the West and someone from the Maritimes; someone from Quebec and someone from Ontario. A female. Someone who knew the ropes in Ottawa. Someone who knew the substance of what was being attempted. The names of the board members not mentioned below and a comment on each appear in Appendix A.

As a board, they met only twenty-six times in four years and then it was to ratify the decisions of the five-member Executive Committee to whom they had delegated the decision-making authority. It was this group, under the chairmanship of John Fisher or Georges Gauthier and sometimes both, who were ultimately responsible for the success or failure of the Centennial festivities. The members of the Executive Committee made a well-balanced team. They were:

- Philip T. Davis, Ottawa, in the lumber and building supply business, was shrewd, incisive, fair-minded and diligent; he brought all his business skills to bear on the Committee's decisions most successfully.
- Ernest A. Côté, deputy minister of the Department of Northern Affairs and Natural Resources, was patrician, wise and fair. An Edmonton Côté and a true professional public sector executive, his experience was invaluable because he knew the government system intimately.
- Dr. John S. Hodgson, Ottawa, assistant deputy minister, Department of National Defence, who appeared destined to become a senior of seniors, sustained the link to Cabinet and Treasury Board with great effectiveness.

- Mrs. Marianne Linnell, Vancouver, B.C., alderman and a real estate agent, was an effective representative of the West Coast ethos.
- A.R. Micay, Q.C., Winnipeg, prototypical of the Winnipeg elite, he brought to the table all the best aspects of that durable, multicultural society, combined with a lawyer's sense of fairness and respect for procedure.

They met month after month, seventy-two times from March 30, 1963, to October 31, 1967, their only remuneration out-of-pocket expenses, their only motivation to serve their country well.

It is hard to imagine a more effective and efficient group.

Their function was one of reviewing program and project proposals coming in from the secretary, the branch directors and the subordinate officers. It was a hierarchical form of organization. Position papers were produced by staff, setting out the subject, issue or problem. The pros and cons were laid out, a conclusion was reached and a recommendation made, often with a choice of action and generally with the preferred choice indicated. A budget was included. What the lawyers would call due diligence was applied in every case. Good staff work. The papers may have been prepared by the staff but they were signed by either the secretary, Director of Planning Robbins Elliott, myself or one of the other branch directors — the ones who were responsible for the recommendations. But the Executive Committee, the board and ultimately the minister, could be held accountable.

Following approval, the proposals, often with revisions requested by the Executive Committee, would, in cases involving expenditures in excess of $25,000, be transformed into submissions to Treasury Board, which is a committee of the Cabinet and the general manager of the government. Once a submission had passed this checkpoint, funds could be expended. But no large amounts could be spent without this level of approval. (Note: All dollar references are 1967 dollars.)

The procedure by which each program would be implemented was left to the discretion of the staff and to the judgement of the branch director to see that all elements were carried out according to acceptable norms of probity, practicality, economy and political sensibility. This is the stuff of management and administration. It worked well. There were few hitches and no scandal.

As mentioned earlier, the board and Executive Committee did not operate in a vacuum. They reported to one Cabinet minister and were thus ultimately accountable to Cabinet and the prime minister. From 1963 to 1965 the secretary of state (the minister responsible for the Centennial Commission) was Maurice Lamontagne, a Quebec intellectual who was president of the Privy Council from April 22, 1963, to February 3, 1964, and secretary of state from that date to December 16, 1965. Lamontagne was a foil for Prime Minister Lester B. Pearson who, like many Anglophone PMs before him realized that it was essential to have a lieutenant from Quebec. The minister had been educated at Laval University in Quebec City and gone on to do graduate work at Harvard. He was an economist and professor, first at Laval and then at the University of Ottawa. When Lester B. Pearson was in Opposition, Lamontagne had been his principal advisor on Quebec-related issues. He was a federalist (not a Quebec nationalist) who promoted the concepts of biculturalism and bilingualism — and was as close as it is possible to being bicultural himself. (One can become flawlessly bilingual with study and practice, but it is much more difficult to become bicultural. For most, one culture will dominate, subordinating the other. It is therefore rare to find persons who are perfectly bicultural.)

Biculturalism was high on the agenda of the Centennial, since it was important for the festivities to give Quebec a sense of historical belonging. It was therefore logical to designate Lamontagne's ministry responsible for the Centennial. The Centennial of Confederation observances appeared to be a neat fit — for him and for the office he headed, secretary of state.

Was he a good minister? Was he good for the Centennial? He made three major contributions. He arranged for the change in the legislation that overcame the word "National" in the name.

The original Act had called us the National Centennial Administration, but since Quebec thinks of itself as a nation and of Confederation as a political, rather than a national, event, the term "National" was offensive to Quebec. So we became the Centennial Commission. Lamontagne also dreamed up the expensive Confederation Memorial Program that left a lot of impressive hardware in each of Canada's provincial capitals. His third contribution, probably the most important one, was that he skilfully and gently sorted out problems that the provincial Centennial ministers encountered as they tried to mesh with the federal operations. His executive assistant from that period recalls many quiet luncheons, telephone calls and one-on-one meetings where Lamontagne's decency and soft manner untied knots and smoothed passages.

He privately and publicly disapproved of Fisher, a serious circumstance, since Fisher was in effect Lamontagne's deputy. Fisher was able to defend himself, but his credibility was seriously damaged in the eyes of official Ottawa as a result. In consequence, until Georges Gauthier's appointment as associate commissioner, the staff suffered a disadvantage — the stigma of Fisher — in dealing with the central government agencies, particularly the Treasury Board.

As soon as Gauthier was in place, however, Lamontagne behaved like a tame pussycat. He signed everything presented to him, gave no leadership and made no proactive moves. For the employees of the Commission, for whom he was the minister, that was just fine. Lamontagne made his contribution, but he did not make a big splash. His field was economics. He had nothing in his formation that allowed him to teach "celebration."

He was forced to resign from the Cabinet and the government on December 16, 1965, over a "scandal" about some furniture bought on credit. The deal was perceived to have created a sense of obligation to help somebody politically, a person who was involved in the transaction. The prevailing view was that it was not only unfortunate but unnecessary. "Witch hunt" and "scapegoat" were the words on the lips of his supporters and of objective observers.

His successor as secretary of state was an entirely different cat. Julia Verlyn "Judy" LaMarsh was extremely colourful and the antithesis of phlegmatic. She was a perfect choice as minister responsible for the Centennial celebration, although the circumstances of her appointment were, from her standpoint, inauspicious: she was plucked out of a very senior post as minister of the Department of National Health and Welfare to become secretary of state, viewed as junior in the pecking order.

While Lamontagne had trouble getting elected and never did appear to have the politician's flair or to possess the royal jelly, LaMarsh swamped her opponents in the riding of Niagara Falls in the elections of 1960 and 1963.

She was a lawyer, a small and big "l" Liberal and a politician through and through. She was only the second woman in Canadian federal political history up to that time to occupy a Cabinet post. Although her name suggested "bicultural" and "bilingual," she was neither. She spoke Japanese better than she spoke French, having taken immersion training during World War II, courtesy of the Canadian Army. But she was very sensitive to Quebec's feelings and aspirations and counted her French-speaking colleagues in the Cabinet among her best friends. It also helped that Judy had a pioneering spirit, an original mind and a good sense of fun. She was the perfect minister to preside over the nationwide mega-anniversary.

Apparently tireless (though often fatigued), Judy hosted heads of state, presided with flair and relish at opening and closing ceremonies and gave visible support to the "troops" who worked so hard to make the Centennial year a success. She was a good example, a good Canadian, a good politician, a good minister and a good woman. She had power and knew how to use it.

She was given advice by the National Conference on Canada's Centennial, the advisory body that had swallowed the Canadian Centenary Council. It consisted of sixty members appointed by the minister from across Canada, including at least two members from each of the ten provinces, appointed on the recommendation of the provincial governments. Meetings were held twice a year.

The National Conference was a reactive body, not a proactive one, so, it was never a source of ideas. The plan seems to have been to protect the government politically so it could say, "Everyone had a hand in what we're doing." From that standpoint it was a reasonable concept.

It also provided a federal-provincial network and links among the plural elements of the Canadian reality that proved useful. The usefulness did not come out of the two meetings a year, but rather from the one-on-one relationships that resulted from the meetings between Commission staff, the minister, and among the members.

A think tank, an intellectual brew from which commendable ideas might be distilled would have been welcomed but while the elements for such a structure were present in the National Conference, it did not function in this manner.

The meetings of the National Conference became show-and-tell affairs, since there was nothing for them to do but nod assent. Eventually, the body came to be viewed as an expensive waste of everyone's time. Perhaps it provided a motivation to get ideas dressed up for presentation on a regular, if infrequent, schedule. Although that may have justified its existence in the early years, in 1966 and 1967, there was no more show and tell to do — the whole thing had already been displayed.

The minister, who was the chairman, lost interest in the group, and it devolved upon Fisher to figure out what to do with them. This was great stuff for him with his penchant for publicity.

The final series of meetings were mere junkets with no purpose. The most memorable was one in which, at Fisher's suggestion, a hundred-seat passenger plane was chartered to take the group to the Arctic Circle. Yes, the Arctic Circle! This was designed to eat up the three days allotted for the meeting. And it did.

Fisher had hired a publicist to get some ink and air time out of the junket, but she ran off with one of the provincial cabinet

CHAP. 60

An Act respecting the Observance of the
Centennial of Confederation in Canada.

[Assented to 29th September, 1961.]

HER Majesty, by and with the advice and consent of the Senate and House of Commons of Canada, enacts as follows:

SHORT TITLE.

1. This Act may be cited as the *National Centennial Act.*   Short title.

INTERPRETATION.

2. In this Act,   Definitions.
- (a) "Administration" means the National Centennial Administration referred to in section 3;   "Administration."
- (b) "Commissioner" means the Commissioner of the Administration;   "Commissioner."
- (c) "Conference" means the National Conference on Canada's Centennial referred to in section 17;   "Conference."
- (d) "Deputy Commissioner" means the Deputy Commissioner of the Administration;   "Deputy Commissioner."
- (e) "director" means a director of the Administration;   "Director."
- (f) "Fund" means the National Centennial Fund established by this Act;   "Fund."
- (g) "member" means a member of the Conference; and   "Member."
- (h) "Minister" means the Prime Minister of Canada or such other member of the Queen's Privy Council for Canada as is designated by the Governor in Council.   "Minister."

PART I.

CONSTITUTION OF ADMINISTRATION.

3. There shall be a corporation to be called the National Centennial Administration consisting of a Commissioner, a Deputy Commissioner and not more than eight directors each of whom shall be appointed by the Governor in Council to hold office during pleasure.   National Centennial Administration.

Centennial flame-lighting ceremony: Prime Minister Lester B. Pearson, Secretary of State Judy LaMarsh, and the Honourable Jean Marchand, with mayors and reeves of the National Capital Region municipalities behind them

(BILL OLSON/DOMINION-WIDE/NATIONAL ARCHIVES OF CANADA/C–26964)

Centennial symbol flag   (NATIONAL ARCHIVES OF CANADA/PA–185473)

The Honourable Maurice Lamontagne, P.C., secretary of state 1963–1965. Minister responsible for the Centennial Commission during the initial years
(Duncan Cameron/National Archives of Canada/PA–115172)

The Honourable Judy LaMarsh, secretary of state and minister responsible for federal Centennial Affairs
(National Archives of Canada/PA–185466)

Dr. N.A.M. MacKenzie,
president of the Canadian
Centenary Council and
member of the board of
directors of the
Centennial Commission
(FRED S. SCHIFFER/NATIONAL ARCHIVES
OF CANADA/PA–185518)

Dr. John S. Hodgson,
member of the Executive
Committee of the board of
directors of the Centennial
Commission   (NATIONAL FILM
BOARD OF CANADA/NATIONAL ARCHIVES
OF CANADA/PA–185477)

"Mr. Canada," John Wiggans Fisher, commissioner of the Centennial Commission and chairman of the board of directors (Centennial Commission Photo/National Archives of Canada/PA–185524)

Robert Choquette, the "Prince of Poets." Originally appointed deputy commissioner of the Centennial Commission; left in 1964 to become Canadian Consul-General in Bordeaux, France (National Archives of Canada/PA–167772)

Georges Gauthier, associate commissioner, Centennial Commission (NATIONAL FILM BOARD/NATIONAL ARCHIVES OF CANADA/PA–185481)

Robbins Elliott, director of the Planning Branch, Centennial Commission (MALAK/NATIONAL ARCHIVES OF CANADA/PA–185521)

Claude Gauthier, secretary of the Centennial Commission
(Tsin Van/National Archives of Canada/PA–185482)

Jean-Pierre Houle, initially appointed director of public relations, later became director of research, Centennial Commission (Dominion-Wide/National Archives of Canada/PA–185478)

John Fisher, centre, proudly displays his giant-sized gavel to his initial Centennial Commission team. Left to right: Robbins Elliott, Peter H. Aykroyd, Claude Gauthier, Robert Choquette, Jean-Pierre Houle

Chester F. Prevey, financial advisor and director of administration, Centennial Commission

Centennial Medal: About 20,000 Canadians were awarded the Canadian Centennial Medal, on the recommendation of a committee headed by Ernest Steele, undersecretary of state.
(CANADIAN PRESS.1967)

Mrs. Marie Callahan, 63-year-old Parliament Buildings maintenance staff member, was amazed to find a Centennial Medal in her mailbox. After 27 years of perfect attendance at her job, she earned the medal "in recognition of valuable service to the nation." (THE OTTAWA CITIZEN STAFF PHOTO, NOVEMBER 22, 1967)

The Centennial coins designed by Alex Colville: $20 gold piece, 1/2 ounce pure gold; Canada Goose silver dollar; wolf 50-cent coin; wildcat 25-cent coin; mackerel 10-cent coin; rabbit 5-cent coin; dove 1-cent coin (ROYAL CANADIAN MINT/NATIONAL ARCHIVES OF CANADA/PA–185468)

Delegates to the Charlottetown Conference from the Legislatures of Canada, New Brunswick, Nova Scotia and Prince Edward Island, September 1, 1864
(G.P. Roberts/National Archives of Canada/C–733)

Joey Smallwood, premier of Newfoundland, in Charlottetown in 1964, with actors who re-created the Charlottetown Conference of 1864 (DOMINION-WIDE/NATIONAL ARCHIVES OF CANADA/PA–185512)

National Committee meeting held May 12, 1965, at the Hotel Saskatchewan, Regina. Seated, from left to right: Hon. J.W. Gardiner, Regina, Sask.; Hon. Maurice Lamontagne, secretary of state; M. Lucien Darveau, c.r., P.Q. Standing, left to right: M. Norbert Préfontaine, Canadian Centenary Council; Mr. John Fisher, commissioner of the Centennial Commission; Hon. Alfred Monnin, St. Boniface, Man.; Dr. Bruce Fergusson, Halifax, N.S.; Hon. J.R. Chalker, St. John's, Nfld.; Hon. James Auld, Toronto, Ont.; Hon. W.D. Black, Victoria, B.C.; Hon. David Stewart, Charlottetown, P.E.I.; Hon. Henry Irwin, Fredericton, N.B.; Hon. Ambrose Holowach, Edmonton, Alta.; Mr. G. Giannou, St. John's, Nfld.

Crowd lined up to enter the Centennial caravan, Richmond Hill, Ontario

Madame Georges Vanier waves goodbye as the Confederation train leaves Ottawa Union Station, bound for the official beginning of the train's tour from Victoria on January 9, 1967. (DOMINION-WIDE/NATIONAL ARCHIVES OF CANADA/PA–185505)

Centennial train, Vancouver, British Columbia (NATIONAL ARCHIVES OF CANADA/PA–183654)

Leslie Maiden, chief of Confederation Train and Caravan Division, Centennial Commission
(JOHN EVANS/NATIONAL ARCHIVES OF CANADA/PA–185499)

Her Majesty Queen Elizabeth, accompanied by Secretary of State Judy LaMarsh, walks along a raised platform on Parliament Hill after viewing the Folk Arts Festival
(MALAK/NATIONAL ARCHIVES OF CANADA/PA–185507)

Aerial view of the Confederation caravans going through their training manoeuvres, Centralia, Ont. (CENTENNIAL COMMISSION PHOTO/NATIONAL ARCHIVES OF CANADA/PA–185502)

Centennial caravan
(NATIONAL ARCHIVES OF CANADA/PA–183646)

Centennial Commission board of directors, 1965. From left to right: Marianne Linnell, A.R. Micay, John S. Hodgson, Norman MacKenzie, John Fisher, P.T. Davis, Hugh O. Mills, Georges Gauthier, Ernest A. Côté
(MAURICE CROSBY/NATIONAL ARCHIVES OF CANADA/PA–185483)

Left to right: John Fisher, Centennial commissioner and chairman of the board of directors; the Hon. Judy LaMarsh, secretary of state; Mr. Georges Gauthier, Centennial associate commissioner and first vice-chairman
(DOMINION-WIDE/NATIONAL ARCHIVES OF CANADA/PA–185472)

members, deplaning at Whitehorse in the Yukon, never to be seen again.

One of the citizen-inspired Centennial projects was the construction in St. Paul, Alberta, of a landing pad for UFOs, and this provided the locus for another eat-up-time meeting of the National Conference. An Armed Forces *Chinook* helicopter was requisitioned to take the group there and after the entymologically shaped flying object had put down daintily on the pad, a meeting was held then and there, at this auspicious site with all its attendant chimerical expectancy.

The National Conference was useful for one thing, however. The membership included two people from each of the ten provinces — the minister responsible for Centennial affairs in each province plus his deputy. This group known as the National Committee became a substructure within the Conference, consulting with each other during meetings of the National Conference, as well as separately. This structure was essential in order to define common objectives, and to co-ordinate the national program of the Centennial Commission with those activities that were provincially sponsored. This group received no publicity, but by its work throughout the period 1963-67, a smooth blend of activities was made possible and potential conflicts were avoided. Centennial year would not have been entirely successful without it.

Now Fisher had a Commission, an advisory body and a National Committee of ministers and deputies but nobody to do this Centennial job. In February 1963, he began to cast around for competent staff to execute the gargantuan task that lay ahead.

Employee number one was Claude Gauthier (no relation to Georges Gauthier), a slender man with aquiline features and a pleasant manner. He was correspondence secretary in the prime minister's office. Trained in the manner of a seminarian, fluently bilingual, charming, diplomatic, intelligent, politically astute, even cute in the sense that he was clever and shrewd, he was appointed assistant to the commissioners and secretary of the Commission on March 11, 1963. He was an executant, one who carries out the wishes of his superior, but not in the sense that he receives delegated authority. There is a difference. Claude Gauthier knew this difference and performed a difficult and onerous job flawlessly and with apparent ease.

The second appointment was Leo LaFrance, hired on March 25, 1963. His function was logistical. He had to find office space and set up a rudimentary infrastructure so the Centennial Administration, as the Commission was called in the beginning, could start functioning. He was part of the support staff in the Privy Council Office and was one of a handful of people who were made available to perform this function for Royal Commissions and other entities that were having to make a flying start from zero.

He had the instincts of the regimental sergeant-major — a sort of one-man light-aid detachment — and he was a wizard at his job. Office space? Furniture? Telephone and telephone listing? Supplies? Switchboard operator? A picture of the Queen and Philip? A water cooler? A coffee maker? Whatever. He was Mr. Jump-Start. Plus, like the modern InstaBank — cash to get going? No problem. How much?

Leo LaFrance (who spoke no French) was a dream walking for John Fisher. He had recently set up the Royal Commission on Banking and had remained as administrative officer. He clearly had visions of remaining with the Centennial organization as combined chief of personnel and finance, but it became apparent very soon that the Centennial was *une autre paire des manches* as his great-great-grandfather might have said (or another kettle of fish as he would have said). Early staff forecasts were producing the need for hundreds of employees, and financial forecasts envisioned disbursement of over $100 million. Appendix B describes something of the budgeting process.

There is a great gulf between sergeant-major and colonel and it was evident that it was the latter that was needed. Leo unplugged himself from the accelerating Centennial energy in late 1963 and went off to crank up yet another Royal Commission in need of his special talent in overcoming stubborn inertia.

It was Chester F. Prevey from Victoria, B.C., who eventually took up the challenge later in 1963. A good-natured, diligent administrator, he saw the task through to conclusion with the assistance of a very small staff.

The second senior staff appointee following Claude Gauthier was Robbins Elliott, transmogrified from lobbyist to doer. Robbins had been an officer in the Canadian Army serving in Europe (1941-45) and later was executive assistant to The Honourable Robert Winters when he was minister of public works in Louis St. Laurent's government, and as stated earlier, was executive director of the Royal Architectural Institute of Canada at the time of his appointment. Robbins came well prepared since he had been chairman of the Program Research Committee of the Canadian Centenary Council, therefore bringing with him a distillation of all the program and project thought that had gone on in the CCC over the last three years or so.

He was named director of planning on May 31, 1963, a title he held until the end. In 1965-66, planning segued to operations, but he was too busy to change his title on the organization chart. And because modesty was one of the characteristics of this upright and assiduous man, perhaps he didn't care.

The third appointment, made concurrently, was Jean-Pierre Houle as director of public relations and information. A very civil, even courtly person, he had been a respected radio broadcaster in Montreal, but unfortunately turned out to be out of his element in a federal agency. He lacked the ability to think big and to macro-plan, and was probably frustrated by the Anglo atmosphere of Ottawa. At the time, nearly all government departments and central agencies operated in English, and the Centennial Administration slipped into this mode from the start, with no effective complaint from the Francophones. Houle was profoundly uncomfortable, unable to show his full abilities because of the language barrier. His pain was obvious.

Jean-Pierre, submitting the budget for print in the fiscal year 1963-64 actually reduced the amount from his budget for the previous year, from $21,000 to $18,000 (the aggregated dollar spent on print eventually reached an estimated $6.5 million). At a meeting of the board in 1964, Fisher, in a shocking display, pilloried Jean-Pierre mercilessly in front of the board and the staff, and summarily dismissed him from his post. Fisher, after all, was Mr. Canada. Public relations was his métier, even though it was often himself he was puffing. Here he had a director of public relations who thought that $18,000 was all that was needed for print, and the Centennial only three years away. A proud man, and with good reason to be, this public humiliation shattered Houle, and although he was appointed director of research (a position with ill-defined function and with a staff of only his faithful secretary Miss C. de Grandmont and one clerk), he was neutralized and contributed negligibly to the rapidly expanding national Centennial effort.

The fourth senior staffer was myself. My interest in the impending Centennial had been aroused in December 1961 by the publicity generated by the Canadian Centenary Council. The knee-jerk, compulsive, no-choice-but-to-do-something syndrome began its motivating power in me. There are a lot of "I's" in the next few pages but how else can one tell a personal story?

I was, at the time, director of the Information and Historical Division of the National Capital Commission (NCC) in Ottawa, the federal government body whose mandate is to see that the seat of the government of Canada is developed and maintained in a manner in keeping with its national significance. This, translated into action, means making the National Capital Region a spectacular place to live. But another theme is clearly present, and that is the theme of Canadian national pride.

I had made a tour of all the Canadian provinces, sponsored by the Canadian Club, speaking on this very subject, so national boosterism had become part of my character. I had also been responsible for the formation of an Historical Advisory Committee, under the chairmanship of Anthony Adamson, who was at the time arguably Canada's foremost proponent of architectural conservancy. Our work included the plans for a proposed Centennial project relating to the restoration of

Richmond Landing, Victoria Island and the Thompson Mill, a kind of historic park. My reasoning was that if I could move into this Centennial thing, it might be a natural evolutionary step in my career that would get me out of parochial Ottawa and onto the national scene.

The psychology of ambition was at work, and more subtly, the psychology of narcissism. I had enjoyed the plaudits of Canadian Club audiences, liked being the spokesman for the NCC, revelled in the radio, TV and newspaper interviews. I needed appreciation. How many politicians, actors, singers and athletes — all performers in fact — are propelled forward in their careers by this often disguised, unrecognized need? How many drops of water make the ocean? So I sought out John Fisher in early April 1963 and said I would like to help him.

"But a committment has been made to fill all the senior positions," he replied.

"Well, let's create a new position, a slot for a new director."

"What do you suggest?"

"How about director of special projects? I'll find some special projects — heaven knows enough of them are being suggested."

I liked Fisher. *Charisma* may be a little strong, but he had something akin to it. Charisma comes from the Greek *charis*, a gift. He was gifted. I sensed that he liked me. I did not know it at the time, but he had a deep distrust of French Canadians (a deplorable trait for one heading up the national celebrations, but a fact nonetheless). He was stuck with Robert Choquette and may not have had much to do with the selection of Claude Gauthier. Robbins Elliott was viewed as a partisan Liberal (by the time I approached Fisher, the Liberals were back in power), and he may have seen me as someone who would have been his own choice in the first place. I had bona fides as a professional engineer, as a patriot, and as one with a history orientation. And I was a WASP from Toronto. I was also a professional public sector manager with postgraduate work in administration, history and public law. He may have innately sensed the narcissistic thing and the subtle bond inherent in that. We hit it off.

I appeared before the board a few weeks later, spoke with evident passion about Canada, showed them the NCC Centennial project and responded in French to questions from Choquette and Côté as they gently assayed that dimension of my *baggage*. They created a new position, director of special projects, and I became the fourth and last of Fisher's senior line officers, the date on the appointing order-in-council being May 31, 1963.

At the board interview Fisher asked me what I thought should be done by way of a Centennial program. He asked specifically was I of the "Eiffel Tower School." I knew about Alexandre Gustave Eiffel and his 984-foot tower built as the tallest building in the world to mark the 1889 centennial of France becoming a republic. I was not of that school. I said I thought the celebrations should be distributed, participatory. It could be argued that the Eiffel Tower has done its job well. It certainly is a viable route. But it only does part of the job.

Robbins was perplexed and disturbed by my appointment. As director of planning, he knew innately that he would have programs and projects to run as well. After all, he had not been attracted to this effort just to plan and then leave. What did "special projects" mean? Weren't all the Centennial projects special? The inclination to protect turf started early. But he had nothing to fear: a natural and logical boundary soon developed, and I never did trespass on his expanding and pre-eminently important territory.

One name that never appeared in the official record was John de B. Payne. A Montreal-based, much consulted and internationally respected expert on Quebec affairs, he was on the executive of the Liberal Party of Canada and as such was on a first-name basis with all the Cabinet ministers, from the prime minister down. Almost from Day 1, I retained John de B. Payne on a subcontract from a freelance PR operator in Ottawa named Glenn Gilbert.

He was my rabbi, in the New York police department sense. Today he would be called a mentor, but he was more than that. He would keep me informed of what all of official Ottawa was thinking — who was in, who was out, and who was coming in and going out. J. Edgar Hoover would have been proud to have had such an operative. One phone call to John on a tricky question of policy formulation or on a sticky relationship that was developing would bring an informed, wise and helpful response. For over three years the monthly retainer paid to him through Gilbert literally saved my life and possibly my career. He gave me confidence to venture into dangerous waters and if I was undecided about proceeding, he would either directly or indirectly provide me with the guidance I required. He knew where the rapids were. He knew what I could get away with.

None of my peers or staff knew of this hidden strength. Fisher was vaguely aware of it and Georges Gauthier turned Nelson's blind eye.

Georges' sly smile often said, "You know that I know, and I know that you know that I know."

It wasn't intrigue. It was just subtle politics, or invaluable intelligence. Rabbi and mentor. My education prospered mightily from the substance behind the monthly Gilbert invoices that read "For Services Rendered."

The senior officers were all in place by June 1, 1963, but the Commission was still without an infantry to carry out the mountain of tasks required to get the celebrations going. In hiring, the secretary and branch directors were faced with one difficulty. Although a job with the Centennial administration could be seen as a once-in-a-lifetime opportunity, it could also be seen as a dead-end street. All Centennial jobs would, of course, disappear at the end of 1967. An absolute, ineluctable sunset, with not a scintilla of hope that the sun would ever shine like this again.

Many excellent managers and administrators would naturally shun employment in such a circumstance. Upward mobility arrested for what? Those who may have been attracted through the secondment route may have made the same realistic appraisal. They would have had no interest in working for the Centennial Commission and returning to their old organization when it was all over. Their peers would have forged ahead and they would have lost precious opportunities for advancement.

So with whole cadres of potential candidates unavailable, from whence could managers and administrators be recruited? Opportunism brought some people in — generally from outside government. It looked pretty good to them. The unemployed also applied, since, after all, a job is a job. There were contract employees and beneficiaries of patronage. (It was a swell place for the minister to parachute in the "deserving" faithful.) There was also a smattering of idealists who saw a once-in-a-lifetime chance to do something worthwhile. And finally, there were the "halt, the lame and the blind" — not quite, but there were a few otherwise unemployables who managed to get aboard.

If they were warm bodies, could hear thunder and see lightning, they were considered. Staff seemed to be attracted to us. We did not have to go looking.

Among those who came seeking work were a group of excellent professional personnel, emanating from one source — the Armed Forces. Since Canadian military policy requires mandatory retirement at age fifty-five, every year a large cohort of army, navy and air force officers has to call it quits. Most of them are experienced, knowledgeable, fit and disciplined. And available!

On the face of it, one would have reason to doubt that anything could be run by such a potpourri of personnel. But all pulled together against the common enemy: the swiftly passing days, the looming immovable deadline set in stone by the calendar.

The opportunists showed what they could do with an opportunity. The contract employees, most with excellent skills, showed their stuff. The unemployed and the unemployable, perhaps out of gratitude, did their best, which in most cases wasn't too bad. The idealists inspired the others and expended prodigious efforts themselves. And the military treated it like warfare (time, the enemy). They knew about strategy and tactics in combat.

Of this latter group, one seasoned bureaucrat remarked that the Navy officers were best suited to tasks requiring diplomacy, the Air Force to tasks requiring innovation and with a technical aspect, the Army officers to jobs involving organization and logistics.

One final factor. The Centennial celebration was a decentralized affair. We had to find a mechanism to co-ordinate activities, all of which, apart from the program in the capital, were taking place outside of Ottawa. It became necessary to appoint Centennial Commission liaison officers in each region, since events were province-specific or city-specific. At first we had trouble believing that such a structure was necessary, but it was forced on us when the need for co-ordination became pressing.

Regional officers had little authority but much responsibility, a very difficult situation in which to work. But they performed with goodwill, and time and again rescued us from conflicts, soothed hurt feelings, opened doors for project officers and headquarters staff. Functionally, they were encouraged and permitted to contact directly any officer at Centennial Commission headquarters in Ottawa and for administrative purposes reported to the secretary of the Commission.

Experts in administrative practice might shake their heads in disbelief. But believe it or not, it worked. Staffing started in 1963, slowly building month by month, until a critical mass of 230 was reached in late 1966 and all systems were go. It was a combined operation. And it worked.

The staffing process that was followed was typical "muddling through." The government had a well-respected Public Service Commission quite able to field lists of potential candidates, but as neither of the two commissioners had any government experience and the first employee, Leo LaFrance, was relatively junior, no approach was made to the PSC. It might have been wise for all of us to have used them, but on the other hand that would have involved getting tied up in their rigorous procedures and valuable time would have been lost.

If there is a moral to be found here it is: Start early and use to the maximum your human resource department. At the same time, however, keep control of the hiring and get authority in writing to bring unorthodox people on board, in unorthodox ways if necessary.

CHAPTER *5*

Of Gifts, Monuments and Memorials

W HEN STAFFING WAS STILL IN its early stages, we knew we had to come up with a program — but what kind of a program? The most logical place to look for direction was of course, the Centennial Act, but that piece of legislation had been put together by legislative draftsmen in the Department of Justice, and like any group of lawyers trying to serve a client, these legal experts had simply tried to catch the general drift of what the government wanted and then put it in lawyerly language. The tendency is to be general, and let the plain English or French words speak for themselves.

The Act created the Centennial Administration (later the Centennial Commission) and then gave us some plain words to interpret in whatever way we chose. The word *promote* was there. A good choice of words — you have to get people interested. The word *plan* was there. Of course, we had to plan, but what? The word *implement* was there. Another good word, but no detail. All these fine words were modified by the phrase "...in order that the Centennial may be observed throughout Canada in a manner in keeping with its national and historical significance." In this simple phrase lay three of the precepts listed in *The Anniversary Axiomatique:* the principle of unification — the celebrations were to take place throughout Canada, and the provision of continuity and restatement, reminding people of the past that shapes the present. All to be observed.

The Act went on to give us permission to get involved with any province or organization with objectives similar to ours. And, oh yes, we could give them money. This money was to come from a Centennial fund, but its use was restricted to big capital projects, which usually take a long time to build. For the year-to-year funding of other projects and activities, we were told in legal language to come cap in hand to Treasury Board every year with an annual budget justifying our requests.

In matters of public policy of a cardinal nature, the British and the Canadian practice is to have a Royal Commission study the subject area, to report and then have drafted a White Paper setting out the desired course of public policy. After Parliamentary debate this White Paper evolves into an Act of Parliament or an executive guideline to the government department concerned.

Some preliminary work of this nature is essential if governments, institutions and corporations are to inject optimum efficiency and effectiveness in their reaction to the anniversary syndrome. Had the government done something little like this before setting up the Commission, the whole program might have been improved.

In the preamble to the prose describing the Record Group 92, which is the Centennial Commission material in the National Archives of Canada, there is a reference to interdepartmental meetings in November 1959, and of an inaugural meeting of provincial ministers on February 8, 1960, so some preliminary soundings were made. But there is no record of these soundings in the archives, so it is difficult to comment on their efficacy.

Our task would have been easier if we had been provided with a set of precepts with an indication of what percentage of funds and effort should be spent on what elements. It would also have been helpful to have access to survey results indicating what level of interest we might expect in Quebec and the rest of Canada, and to have a budget with an upper and lower limit.

We had none of these. There was no indication of how much money the government was prepared to spend or, indeed, what level of interest there might be among Canadians *a mare usqui ad mari*. The lack of a public opinion poll in Quebec was a glaring lacuna. If we had focused on engendering the maximum participation of Quebec, we might have altered the course of Canadian history. It was unwise not to have taken this prudent step. Contrary to the advice in *The Anniversary Axiomatique*, we failed to carefully analyze destructive forces and so were in no position to oppose them.

With its open-ended legislative guidelines, the government was really saying, "We'll leave it up to your imagination. See what you can come up with." John Hodgson, who had written the original material that later became the legislation, had emphasized the idea that projects should have lasting significance. He was thus able to interpret the legislation for us. As he was still in the PCO and was now a board member, he offered us a simple administrative guideline for our first program. It was that the government would commit one dollar for every man, woman and child in Canada to be applied to the cost of a Centennial project of lasting significance in every municipality in Canada, provided this dollar was matched by one from the province and one from the municipality.

Put another way, if a local community generated a project of a lasting nature as a permanent memorial to the Centennial of Confederation and the province were to put up a dollar per capita of that community, the federal government would match it. Here we have the concept of gift that is present at all anniversaries. A reward to bring pleasure and happiness. In the anniversary at hand the rewards were to be of a lasting nature — a gift that keeps on giving. The best kind. Within a few days following my appointment, John Fisher handed the one-paragraph gift guideline to me and said, "Here's your first special project."

Such is the life of a public servant. Many a public policy, enunciated initially in spare language, sometimes with internal inconsistencies, and often unrealistic in its objective, is subsequently developed and made effective in circumstances just like this. The process in normal circumstances is that such a policy enunciated by Cabinet would filter down to the deputy minister of one of the great departments of government and he or she would delegate the responsibility for giving it life to a director general or an assistant deputy minister with a span of control of five to ten senior officers and a staff of thousands. But at the Centennial Commission, on the day Fisher gave me this unique blessing, the staff of the Commission numbered seventeen souls and none of them worked for me.

One shorthand way of characterizing the administrative process is the acronym POSDCORB: planning, organization, staffing, direction, co-ordination and budgeting. While each of these is essential, staffing is the most important and it takes a lot of time. You need to write a job description, get approval for the position, advertise for candidates, screen them, check their references, make a selection, get approval for the appointment, accommodate the current schedule of the preferred candidate, get the body in place, indoctrinate and then direct. I had no idea how many bodies would be required for the Centennial Grants Program, but I sensed that the bulk of the work would be done by the provinces.

We had no personnel department, so I went to the Treasury Board myself and requisitioned three positions. While the staffing process ground on at the speed of a glacier, I set about straightening up the inconsistencies and unrealities in the one-paragraph concept that was my mandate, and to design the structures, processes and procedures needed to implement the program. This whole program had become my sole responsibility. Robbins was busy with other planning. Claude Gauthier was busy with his executant function. Fisher was making speeches. Prevey was struggling with the thousand-and-one administrative details of the growing organization. I had to get this thing up and going all by myself.

No philosophy of celebrations was needed to give guidance as to how to structure this program. It was a gift program. I reasoned that the gifts should be appropriate for the occasion and there should be a measure of uniformity throughout Canada. Criteria of a positive nature were developed. The project should preferably be cultural in nature or related to recreation, these two guidelines appearing to be in the spirit of the occasion. However, since a gift should be something the recipient likes, wants or needs, I felt some latitude was required. That is why the word "preferably" was added. The municipalities got the message, as the ensuing analysis of the program results will reveal.

In Canada, however, municipalities are subject to provincial legislation, and the municipality *qua* municipality has no truck nor trade with the federal government. So the funds had to be routed through the provinces, and the qualifying criteria had to be agreed to by the province. All the same, the Centennial Commission, as provider of the funds, had the last word. We did not want one province accepting the reconstruction of Main Street in the guise of a Centennial project when they were going to do it anyway out of road funds. Other provinces could say, "Me too." The same applied to sewage disposal plants. Necessary, but not anniversary in nature, or celebratory or Centennial.

Rome wasn't built in a day, and while permanent memorials in every community in Canada weren't exactly Rome, the old adage had sobering application to our activities. Immediate action was required.

We needed the formal co-operation of each province and the two northern territories (which could come only when each had its own Centennial Act) and we needed assurance that the money was in place to honour the implied commitment. At least $25 million was required from the federal side, and with the co-operation of the Treasury Board (the general managers of the government), the Department of Finance (the bankers for the government), and the minister's office (the one authorized to spend), the money hose was turned on, and in July 1963 the National Centennial Fund was topped up. Robert Choquette obligingly signed the required formal and official correspondence drafted for his signature, quipping about what fun it was to make us instant millionaires.

The first province we zeroed in on was Ontario. It was Canada's most populous province, Centennial interest would likely be high there and relations between Ottawa and Ontario were generally congenial. During a meeting with the provincial treasurer in September 1963, I committed the federal government to provide grants totalling one dollar per capita of the province's population as of June 1, 1963, to help fund Centennial projects. For any given project, the federal contribution was not to exceed one-third of the total cost. Quebec was visited next and then one by one in personal visits to Cabinet members and officials in each province, similar arrangements were made. A slightly different agreement was made with the less prosperous Yukon and Northwest Territories. In those jurisdictions, the federal government was to pay two dollars per capita, up to two-thirds of the cost of each project.

These visits were preceded by letters to each premier from the prime minister of Canada urging the appointment of a provincial minister to be responsible for Centennial affairs and encouraging the passing of concurrent provincial legislation to permit the provinces not only to receive and disburse funds for the Centennial Grants Program but also to co-operate in any other federal programs that might develop. (The letters were drafted by me and approved by the Executive Committee of the Commission and the secretary of state.)

The provinces were highly motivated to co-operate. Here was a ready-made Centennial program that would give them the appearance of "doing something." They were as bewildered about what to do as we were, but they were pleased to be given a financial boost from the national government. Federal-provincial relations were running smoothly at the time, which helped. As usual, there were complaints about the feds and about "Daddy knows best," but being in the carrot-and-stick game was part of the Canadian federalist system of government and it was accepted. It took most of 1963 to get all the provinces lined up and the necessary legislation passed, but

Festival Canada
presents
**STRATFORD
FESTIVAL
COMPANY**

Le Festival du Canada
présente
**LE THÉÂTRE
DU FESTIVAL
DE STRATFORD**

*Examples of advertising material
developed for the Centennial
Commission by Vickers and Benson
Advertising Limited, Toronto;
MacLaren Advertising, Toronto;
and Agence Canadienne, Montreal*

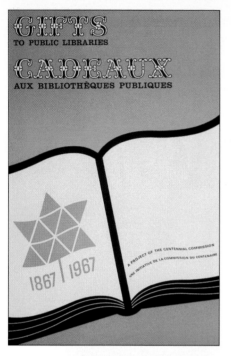

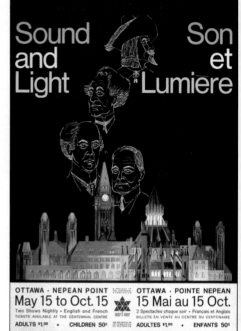

CANADA 1867|1967

Festival Canada presents
Le Festival du Canada présente

NEW YORK PHILHARMONIC
CONDUCTED BY/SOUS LA DIRECTION DE
LEONARD BERNSTEIN

centennial athletic awards

prix d'athlétisme du centenaire

gold
or

silver
argent

bronze
bronze

Centennial Athletic PROGRAMME d'athlétisme du Centenaire

red
rouge

What is Centennial?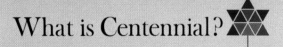

It's the celebration of the 100th anniversary of Canadian Confederation.

It's a time for us to enjoy ourselves—to discover the many wonders of our country, and to contribute in our own way to the most exciting year in our country's history.

It's a time to reflect on past achievements; of our growth into a modern, dynamic country; and to look ahead to a future of prosperity and greatness.

What are you planning for Centennial?

Take this Centennial Symbol

Put it on a banner, use it on your products, and in your advertising, engrave it on your stationery, paint it on your vehicles, wear it on your lapel, display it on your cartons, hang it in your plant or office, stick it on your pay envelopes, stencil it on your coffee cups. Carry it. Fly it. But above all Use it.

The Centennial Commission
P.O. Box 1967
Ottawa, Canada.

Please send me the "Graphics Manual" which explains proper use of the Centennial Symbol.

NAME

COMPANY   TITLE

ADDRESS

THE CENTENNIAL

incrementally, and after countless meetings and lengthy negotiations, a piece of model legislation evolved, and with only minor province-specific amendments, we ended up with a solid cross-Canada legislative framework for all kinds of Centennial activities.

At first, difficulties of interpretation occurred in the grants program — especially when it came to interpreting what was meant by "preferably cultural in nature or related to recreation." Nevertheless, the approval process matured remarkably quickly and the applications coming from the provinces were soon being routinely rubber-stamped. We adopted a totally hands-off attitude regarding the work involved in bringing each project into being but of course urged federal members of Parliament to turn up to add dignity to all official grand openings as they began to occur with increasing frequency in 1967.

After all, we didn't want individual Canadians to forget that the projects were presents from Canada, their country.

The results of the Centennial Grants Program were spectacular. By the end of 1967, more than two thousand projects had been completed in every corner of the country, adding, impressively in a four-year surge, to the recreation and cultural plant of Canada. The only statistical analysis available, while not complete, reveals the scale of the program as at December 31, 1966, when 87 percent of the federal funds had been committed. Appendices C and D show the number of projects by province and the financial contribution of each level of government, and the projects by category, Canada-wide. By looking at the tables, we can draw certain conclusions about the extent to which the programs fit into the anniversary mould.

On the whole, the town fathers (and mothers) displayed good taste and good sense in interpreting the criteria. The loophole "preferably" *was* used, however — and this is revealed in the number of municipal buildings that were constructed or added to. In most of these cases, the heads of the municipal governments likely *needed* new offices or *needed* more room, and as they controlled the application for the matching grants, it was easy to succumb to a self-serving impulse. We resisted these submissions at first, but soon capitulated, reasoning that these structures served the function of a memorial, something made or done in remembrance, and their efficacy in this regard was equal to that of a park, for example. I believe we were right to approve the projects. A psychic need was met; the spirit of celebration was not violated.

The next observation is that different provinces responded in different ways. This was a result of public policy thrusts that differed from region to region, and the influence of the minister responsible for administering the grant program. In Saskatchewan, for example, fifteen senior citizens' homes were constructed, reflecting the caring ethic of the socialist government in that province at the time. In Quebec, where reinforcement of cultural distinction is an ever-present dynamic, of the seventy projects completed, fifty-six were social, recreational or cultural in nature. In British Columbia, a park and recreational thrust was evident — skating rinks, recreational arenas and ski-lifts predominating!

Centennial year was a civilizing year. Look at the projects by category. When the municipal and social services buildings are deleted, all the rest are civilizing elements: 67 museums and art galleries; 428 community centres; 520 recreational structures! In the smaller communities, with shallower tax bases and little commercial or industrial assessment, they did what they could, in the Centennial spirit. (One community bought band instruments; another landscaped the war memorial.) The $100 million of public funds expended on this program was well spent. The anniversary compulsion and Canadian common sense synergized. The result was reassurance, pride and growth. Three of the precepts in *The Anniversary Axiomatique* had come into play: encouraging community improvement, building monuments and memorials and providing future focus.

In February 1964, Fisher received a phone call from Maurice Lamontagne, the minister responsible for the Centennial Commission. The heart of the conversation was this: "I want to give $2.5 million to each of the provinces for a Confederation memorial project. Something big to be built in

each capital. Preferably for a cultural purpose. Look into it."
The idea for this program did not just spring out of thin air. It
had received its impetus, indirectly, from a determined Prince
Edward Island political science professor by the name of
Frank McKinnon. In the late 1950s McKinnon had conducted
a one-man campaign and forceful lobby for the design and
building of a large centre for the performing arts in
Charlottetown, to be called the Fathers of Confederation
Memorial Building. It was a grandiose scheme for a city with
a population of 18,527 in a province with a population of
130,000. The estimated cost of the structure he proposed was
far beyond the financial capability of Prince Edward Island.
Anyway, he argued, the 1864 Charlottetown Conference needed to be commemorated in some way — and what better way
than through the building of this centre? Furthermore, since
the Conference was a Canadian event, Canada should pay.
And Canada did pay. A grant of $2.8 million was made. He
even got contributions from many of the provinces. Everyone
in official Ottawa considered it a potential white elephant, but
it did show that the federal government was willing to play
Centennial ball.

After the Fathers of Confederation Building opened, someone in Quebec must have tweaked Lamontagne by asking,
"How about something for Quebec City, on account of the
Quebec Conference? It was just as important, in fact, it was
more important." Sure enough, there is correspondence dated
November 7, 1963, where the prime minister tells Quebec that
the federal government is prepared to make a grant of $2.8 mil-
lion to help pay for the construction of Le Grand Théâtre du
Québec, in Quebec City. The announcement of this intention
did not receive the publicity accorded the grant made to Prince
Edward Island, but once the decision was made, Lamontagne
quite likely received further tweaking, this time from Cabinet
colleagues from other provinces, saying "Hey, what about us?"
Presto! The Confederation Memorial Program.

Lamontagne had already arranged with the minister of
finance to add an extra $25 million to the Centennial fund, so

we did not have to ask for it, and the legislation was in place for the provinces to receive funds. Thus, the Confederation Memorial Program sprang forth after a very short gestation period and no pain, and another strong bond was forged with the provinces, spurred by Centennial fervour. A guideline was quickly developed:

- The Centennial Commission agrees to contribute to each of the provinces $2.5 million or 50 percent of the cost of construction, whichever is the lesser, toward the cost of a Confederation memorial project to be constructed in each province, preferably for a cultural purpose, and preferably in the provincial capital, in commemoration of the Centennial of Confederation.
- The Commission will contribute $250,000 to each of the two northern territories on a non-matching basis toward the cost of such a project.

The two thousand projects at the municipal level might be considered micro-memorials. Now we had a program of macro-memorials. Gifts to the provinces themselves. Once again the civilizing aspect was present — this time super-civilizing because of the scale.

With the exception of Nova Scotia and New Brunswick, the provinces handled this unexpected Centennial largesse responsibly. Because the mousehole "preferably" had been left for the provinces to crawl into, however, the potential for gross self-serving was present.

Nova Scotia, for instance, had been campaigning for funds for a new medical faculty building at Dalhousie University for some time, and they saw the $2.5 million as just the ticket to put them over the top. Unfortunately, the federal government had put itself in the position of having no veto over a medical building, and rather than fight it or spend time diplomatically attempting to get Nova Scotia to change its mind, they went along with it. Of course, the medical building was what they wanted and needed, but it did not have the civic symbolism of the 174 administration buildings in the other municipal programs. It seemed crass.

New Brunswick presented an even worse case. It took the money and built the Centennial Administrative Building — a plebeian structure to house a lot of government departments that had been scattered in various quarters around Fredericton, the provincial capital. No one in Ottawa felt this was in the Centennial spirit, and it left a bit of a sour taste. Perhaps New Brunswick could not have designed a structure to meet a cultural need in time for a 1967 opening, and rather than forego receipt of the funds, they went for the mundane and the practical.

Other provinces dealt with the issue of "not enough time" in a different way. Many said, "Our memorial will have a cultural purpose all right, but there's no way it can open in 1967." That was all right with us. This program initiative had come along pretty late, so it was not the fault of the provinces that time was running out.

Here's what happened in the other provinces. (In all cases magnificent structures were built and Canada moved up a notch on the "civilized" scale.)

- Newfoundland produced the Centennial Arts and Cultural Centre — the first one ever to be built in that province.
- Ontario constructed the Centennial Centre of Science and Technology (now the Ontario Science Centre) in Toronto — at that time, the most modern science "museum" in North America. The hands-on participation permitted in the exhibits was a welcome new departure.
- In Winnipeg, Manitoba, a new Manitoba Cultural Centre had been constructed but it lacked a concert hall. The construction of that hall became their Confederation memorial project.
- In Regina, Saskatchewan, a proper Performing Arts Centre was constructed, but as Saskatoon was also in need, the funds were split between the two cities and a Saskatoon Centennial Auditorium was constructed.
- In Edmonton, Alberta, a modern museum and archives building was built to house the archival and province-

specific museum material the province had already col-
lected to commemorate its less-than-hundred-year history.

- British Columbia did the same in Victoria, spurred by a
  similar need.
- In the Yukon Territory, the funds provided for a much
  needed Museum of Local History and Civic
  Administration Building in Whitehorse, and in the
  Northwest Territories a Territorial Regional Library was
  constructed in Hay River.

All these projects were designed to help Canadians celebrate
their own cultural achievements and those of others or to look
back at their collective past. All are still standing as reminders
of Canada's year of celebration and as hope for the continuing
development of Canadian culture.

Although the buildings opened a few years after 1967, the
intent of a celebratory gift was nevertheless present. Programs
of this kind are affirming for the citizens who benefit, whether
or not they are received on "the very day." So, if you're
involved in planning turn-of-the-century activities, a good
project should not be refused just because it will not be completed exactly in the year 2000. 1999 is okay and 2001 is okay;
if the project is good, do it!

During the days of the earliest Centennial stirrings, Ottawa,
like the rest of Canada, lacked proper facilities for the enjoy-
ment of the performing arts. The Capitol Theatre on Bank
Street, a 1920s movie house, was the best that could be offered.
The idea of a proper National Arts Centre was floated at that
time, and eventually became thought of as a Centennial project,
but realistically it was recognized that the kind of facility
appropriate for the capital could not be designed and built in
time. It did become a federal project under the direction of the
secretary of state, however, and when it was completed in
1969, it comprised a 2,300-seat hall, the largest stage in Canada,
the largest orchestra pit in Canada, a 900-seat theatre built on
the Elizabethan thrust-stage principle and a 300-seat studio. In
the spirit of the Confederation Memorial Program which provided gifts to the provinces, it was Canada's gift to itself. Over

$4.5 million of Centennial funds went toward the project, the balance of the cost coming from other government votes post-1967. It had the same affirming benefit as the other projects: all Canadians could be proud of it and the 1969 opening did not detract from its suitability as a memorial. The anniversary compulsion produced the political will to do it. It might never have existed otherwise.

An architectural consortium was put together for the express purpose of designing this magnificent facility. The names of the architects reflect Canada's pluralist character: Affleck, Desbarats, Dimakoupoulos, Lebensold and Sise. English, French, Greek and Jewish. A nice creative gene pool. A nice result.

The co-ordinator of the project and later its first director was G. Hamilton Southam, a member of the Southam publishing clan. He took early retirement from his ambassadorial rank position in the Department of External Affairs to devote himself to the cause. Tall and dark, with distinctive and distinguished features, he was urbane, sophisticated, public spirited, an intellectual and an aesthete, and wealthy.

In summarizing the *raison d'être* for the National Arts Centre, he made an eloquent statement that, while not perfectly applicable to all the new cultural buildings that appeared in Canada as a result of the Centennial, is apposite:

> Our actors have practised their art for generations in the misery of high school auditoriums. Our singers have practised theirs in the splendour of European opera houses. The building of the Arts Centre is the most tangible sign, and happily not the only one, that their years of penury and exile are over. Their civilizing influence is at last being recognized, and with recognition and support from the government they are taking the place they deserve in our society. It is not that they have become worthy of our society. It is that our society at last is becoming worthy of them. That surely is the essential meaning of the Arts Centre.

From Joe Batt's Arm in Newfoundland to Eucluelet on the west coast of Vancouver Island, because of the Centennial grants and the Confederation Memorial Program, Canadians could say at the end of 1967 "Hear! Hear!" to the spirit of that statement.

The gifts program was a success. By using existing governmental administrative structures, and trusting in the prudent use of delegated authority, the response of the provincial and municipal governments to the gift aspect of the anniversary compulsion was brilliant.

Do you know about these Centennial Celebrations you'll be able to enjoy in 1967?

967 will be a great year!

Le Train de la Confédération arrive le 24 novembre à Lachine*

Centennial turned out to be the most fun we've had in years!
Were you surprised?

It's as though Canadians had just been waiting for a chance to show how we really feel about this country of ours. Centennial gave us our chance. And from coast to coast we responded with an enthusiasm and delight that's lasting all year long.

Sure, the special projects like the Confederation Train and Caravans are a big success. But it's the personal involvement, the individual participation that has made our Centennial so important. Almost everyone in Canada was involved in the spirit of Centennial.

This is the year we discovered what it means to be Canadian — that we love this land and we're proud of our achievements. We proved we really know how to enjoy being Canadian. And that we're able to show our pride, and faith in the future of our nation.

In 1967, we've learned a l about ourselves as a nation not stop now! Let's enjoy t new knowledge of ourselve make every year to come o excitement and discovery. We'll just call 1968 "Cente Plus One" and keep on goi

The Centennial Commission/Ottawa, Canada.

The Post Office got into the act with the Centennial Definitives 1967–1973, issued August 2, 1967.

CHAPTER 6

Of Symbols and Identity

S
YMBOLS ARE COMMUNICATIVE elements that represent a person, object, group or idea. Every country has its own. Britain has John Bull, the United States has Uncle Sam, France has Marianne and Canada has the Mountie. Every country also has its own flag. Foreigners identify the country by the flag, and citizens of the country identify with it. It's part of their identity. To exalt the flag is to exalt them, to desecrate it is to desecrate them.

The Canadian Centenary Council had been right. The Centennial needed a symbol too. A communicative element that would represent the celebration. This symbol was probably the single most important element required to satisfy the psychic need for unity and reinforcement of identity in the whole mega-anniversary process.

Symbols are an important part of anniversaries, but Canada, at the time of the Centennial preparations, was lacking in any distinctive national symbol. We had a flag, of course, but there was nothing particularly Canadian about it. It was simply a red field with the Union Jack in the upper left quarter — and the Union Jack was the flag of the United Kingdom. It is incredible that a modern state like Canada had no national symbolic signature. This obvious lack was embarrassing to Canadians and their government. Canada was indeed going to show the flag in 1967, but to do that, we needed to *have* a flag.

In 1963 Prime Minister Lester B. Pearson and John Matheson, Liberal MP and heraldic assistant, took some steps to rectify the situation. They promoted a flag with three maple leaves on a white centre square with blue bars on each side. The blue bars were a French blue similar to that used in Quebec for the *fleur de lys*. Diefenbaker's Conservatives favoured the Red Ensign — the original flag, which honoured the British tradition. The NDP opted for a design similar to Pearson's, but with only one maple leaf. The debate, beginning June 15, 1964, was long and loud. A special committee was appointed on September 10 which proposed a suggestion from George F.G. Stanley, Canada's pre-eminent military historian, namely a flag closely resembling that of Canada's Royal Military College in Kingston, Ontario, with red bars on either side and a red maple leaf instead of the college crest in the centre.

A White Paper was tabled in the House of Commons to form the basis of what was to become a long discussion and debate. All members had an opinion about the flag and all wanted a say. The lineup of federal legislation to be debated, including White Papers, is always a long one and the debate did not begin until June 15, 1964. The debate went on for six months and would have gone on longer if it had not been cut off arbitrarily by means of a device called closure.

On December 15, 1964, the new-flag proposal was accepted by 163 votes to 78. On January 28, 1965, Queen Elizabeth proclaimed that the design would become official effective February 15, 1965. Who says symbols are incapable of stirring emotions? Six months' debate in the House of Commons?

THE CENTENNIAL SYMBOL

While Pearson and his political opponents were thrashing out the design of Canada's new flag, the Centennial Commission was busy trying to develop a symbol to represent the Centennial festivities themselves. One of the conditions written into the agreements with the provinces for the Centennial

Grants Program and the Confederation Memorial Program was that the Centennial symbol would be prominently displayed on each project, accompanied by appropriate text indicating the part played by the federal government. But there was no Centennial symbol!

Lo! What is this arising from the mist? Behold! Another Special Project!

There was very little to publicize in 1963 and 1964, and John Fisher particularly was suffering from a paucity of things to talk about. His forté was speaking to captive audiences. If he couldn't do that, Mr. Canada needed to get his hands on something tangible to ease his sense of lack of function.

In late 1963 he called me into his office to discuss the whole subject. The search for a symbol might just become his first *cause*. It would be a great idea to ask the schoolchildren of Canada to design the symbol, he opined; this would build awareness in the asking, in the participation and in the award of the prize to the winner. John got on the phone to his network of newspaper editors, radio and television commentators, and let it be known that Mr. Canada was looking for a symbol for the Centennial. No specifications. Anyone twelve or under could just send in their design before January 1, 1964. All would be considered. The winner would get a tour of Canada, all expenses paid. A brilliant idea, the first crack in the national wall of indifference and unawareness. Let Canadian kids use their imagination.

During my time at the National Capital Commission, I had been responsible for the design of annual reports, pamphlets, booklets and even a full-length book called *The Queen's Choice*. Under the expert tutelage of the eminent Swiss-trained graphic designer, Paul Arthur, I had learned a lot about typography, graphic design and, yes, symbols. I knew John's idea was contrary to the conventional wisdom of how to design a corporate symbol, let alone a symbol for an abstraction like the Centennial of Confederation. But then, the Centennial wasn't conventional.

"I don't want any rules or regulations," he said. "What this is about is awareness. I don't want to inhibit them."

Maybe, just maybe, he was right. But it was more than just common sense that made me feel the idea was misguided. It was instinct. I could smell disaster, delay and ridicule. The design of a symbol for a national festival was a job for a professional not an amateur.

As he was picking up the phone to call the editor of the *Toronto Star* I said, "John, wait. This is a mistake. Let's do this right. Let me get the advice of a professional on how to go about this before you get young Canada involved." John was distracted by an incoming call announcing that a group of native Canadians was in the outer office waiting for an audience. He hung up the phone and said curtly, his face flushed, "All right, go ahead, do it your way. You get us a symbol. But it better be fast and it better be good."

Thus began a drama that lasted the better part of a year. Not fast. And an aborted competition which did not produce a symbol satisfactory to the government. Not good.

It was already symbol time in Canada. Expo '67, the World's Fair to be held in Montreal in 1967, had chosen its emblem in April 1964. *Canadian Art* and *Weekend Magazine* were both running competitions for a design of the Canadian flag. The Canadian Centenary Council had quickly and quietly procured a distinctive symbol of their own. To top it all off, the major debate on the quintessential Canadian symbol, the flag, was to start June 15, 1964.

I wanted to make a success of this Special Project. I wanted to perform impeccably. I wanted to do it right. I placed a call to Paul Arthur. "Paul, please come to Ottawa right away. I want to talk symbols." His advice was crisp, clear and cogent. Run a national competition advertised every place in Canada where a graphic designer might exist, calling for entries with strict specifications attached.

We did just that.

Two thousand calls for entry were mailed out to graphic designers domiciled in Canada, to Canadian graphic designers living abroad, to students specializing in graphic design at art schools and colleges and to Canadian firms operating in the graphic arts field. A jury of respected professionals in the field was chosen, then approved by the minister, and their names were provided with the calls for entry to give confidence to the entrants. Cash prizes would be awarded to the three entries best meeting the design criteria: suitability as a symbol, competence of design and execution, originality of conception, adaptability to many forms of use.

Each entry was to be presented on an 8 x 10 white artboard of a specific weight, executed in black, and bearing a pseudonym in a sealed envelope on the back to avoid judicial prejudice. Acceptance of the cash prize would constitute irrevocable release to the government of all rights to the design. There you have the elements of a perfect competition.

The competition closed on April 10, 1964, in the hope that the winning symbol could be chosen by July 1.

Four hundred and ninety-six entries were judged to have met the conditions. Thirty represented the best of these. The judges submitted their report on judging day, dramatically datelined "Midnight, June 2, 1964."

The first choice was three Cs enclosed on each other with a single maple leaf in the middle. The second was a pair of doves kissing in an avian *pas de deux*, the third a single C with three maple leaves in the middle. When the pseudonym envelopes were opened, it was found that all three were by Quebec designers!

Next morning I proudly displayed the three winners to John. I thought I was so smart. A perfect competition.

He didn't like them. John wanted to involve the female members of the staff in the decision. Having his cohort of sixteen stenographers, secretaries and file clerks do the job would be the democratic and egalitarian way. And staff participation would be good for morale. So we rented the hockey arena at Lansdowne Park, set up trestle tables, laid out all the offerings, gave each of the sixteen female judges three little tags numbered one, two and three, and charged them to deposit the tags face down on their choice for the first-, second-, and third-best of the four hundred and ninety-six designs.

Number three turned out to be the Peace Tower, as a rocket, going straight up in the air with sixty-seven little, round exhaust pipes breathing fire below. Number two was a stylized map of Canada with 1967 scripted in the middle. Number one, by overwhelming choice, was a red-coated Mountie on a black horse at the alert in front of the Peace Tower, with a brown beaver *couchant* in his arms, the beaver holding a sprig of two yellow maple leaves in its mouth. In tiny script, one leaf was marked 1867, the other 1967.

John had to admit his idea hadn't been so hot. The sixteen-member judging committee was diplomatically informed that their preferred choice could not be recommended to the board of directors.

When we did submit the three Quebec designs to the board they liked the three Cs. Then we needed ministerial approval, but the minister thought the approval should come from Cabinet, likely because he was conscious of the flag fever rampant among his colleagues and foresaw a similar controversy erupting over the Centennial symbol.

So on June 24 a memorandum to Cabinet was drafted with a recommendation that the three Cs become the Centennial symbol. But, oh no, on July 2 at a Cabinet meeting all three symbols were rejected. The minister was ordered to suspend everything and to make no announcement about a symbol until the flag issue was settled.

Fisher was so advised, the minister adding, "You may have to get a symbol outside the competition, but don't bring those three designs back to us." You don't disobey that kind of order unless you want an out-of-body experience and see your head rolling down the steps of the Centre Block of the Parliament Buildings.

All that work gone up in smoke. I hadn't been so smart after all. Timing of an excruciatingly unique kind was against us. Back to the proverbially painful, disappointing and humiliating Square One.

Weeks went by as the flag debate droned on. The competition judges were restive and entrants kept calling to see if they'd won. Our vast Centennial network coast to coast kept asking what had happened to the symbol. And since it was generally known that we were looking for a symbol, hopeful and helpful Canadians kept bombarding us with unsolicited suggestions. Offerings arrived almost daily — from Jill McBride in Peggy's Cove, Nova Scotia; from Robert Kruk in Lake Waskesiu, Saskatchewan; from Ricky Thompson in Prince Rupert, British Columbia.

The submissions came in on wrapping paper, waxed paper, aluminum foil, cardboard, and artboard in all colours of the rainbow. They were executed in crayon, pencil, pen, felt-tip marker, and felt strips. One was made of the little coloured sugar pellets used to decorate cakes. Many had been damaged in transit, because of faulty wrapping. One, a salt-and-flour map of Canada, had separated from its wrapping and was delivered unwrapped in three pieces. Eerily enough, Quebec had broken off from the rest of Canada and the Maritimes.

By mid-August the pressure from our constituents was so great that we implored Lamontagne to let us go back to the three Quebec designers and have them modify their designs. We would use the original jury to assist us. This time they would art-direct the work. The minister thought we should go back to the five best in order to give ourselves a few more options.

We put out the word that we couldn't use the three winners because we were having difficulty registering them as trademarks (untrue). How could we tell the real truth? Cabinet had rejected them and said, "Don't bring them back again."

In the days following the minster's directive, it became clear to me that a seven-person jury could not hope to art-direct five designers. It was just impractical, unworkable. So off we went to the Executive Committee, with the recommendation that I be allowed to enter into negotiations with an artist or artists to commission a symbol, that the three winners eventually be paid their prizes and that the public be informed of the miscarriage due to the registration difficulty. This was accepted. I was given a budget of $5,000 to complete the job.

This was one time when I saw Fisher's fury. It was all my fault. Why hadn't he just gone ahead and let the kids design a symbol? What had my smart-ass competition yielded? Nothing. How could he continue to face his friends across Canada; almost 1965 and no symbol. A laughing-stock that's what he'd become. At the end of the tirade (behind closed doors in his office), he growled, "Get us a symbol. Fast."

Back to Paul Arthur. Who's the hottest graphic designer in Canada?

Alan Fleming.

He had designed the corporate symbol for Canadian National Railways and didn't deny the legend that he'd sat at his desk fooling around nervously with a paper clip and bent it unconsciously into an elided C and N, like a single track with curves and straightaways. That was the design. Universally recognized today. CN paid plenty for those nervous two minutes of paper-clip art. It was rumoured that his fee at the time was $50,000. That was $25,000 a minute! Would he come to Ottawa to discuss designing a symbol for us?

He came. We talked. He had actually sketched up some ideas on a barf bag, on the plane to Ottawa. Tentative, nervous thoughts.

What would he charge? $25,000.

When one is in need of a critical operation and wants the best surgeon, one doesn't call for competitive bids. One goes to the best and pays the shot. But $25,000? I had only $5,000. So I told Alan I would think about it. (I kept the barf bag. Too bad it wasn't autographed.)

Back to Paul Arthur again.

What's the hottest design house in Canada that might take this on for $5,000? The Toronto typesetting firm Cooper and Beatty.

So I went to Toronto on October 26. It was a last-chance kind of mission. I had excellent conceptual discussions with Anthony Mann, the creative director, who sensed the situation perfectly. I gave him twenty-two calendar days to present me with one preferred design and one alternate in time for the next board meeting. The idea of a second design was his. It was his experience that committees like to choose, not to be presented with a *fait accompli*. If *prima facie* one design is really better than the other, merit will prevail.

He was given the same specs as those used in the competition. He produced. The two designs were the work of twenty-four-year-old Stuart Ash. One was a stylized maple leaf. The other had a flower motif with ten petals.

November 16. A special informal meeting of the Executive Committee approved the stylized maple leaf, although all agreed it looked like the Star of David. To this Paul Arthur observed, "Everything that is reduced to a simple elemental form is bound to be similar to some other simple elemental form." A handy truism.

November 23. A formal meeting of the Executive Committee ratified the maple leaf.

November 25. The full board of directors viewed the two and ratified the maple leaf.

Then came the final curve that could have struck me out.

The National Conference, the body that was organized by the government to generate ideas, was slated to meet on November 26, and John decided that the designs should be presented to them for a decision. We had just received some top-level professional advice, and we were about to ignore it in favour of the advice of amateurs!

After much argument and pleading, I achieved the best compromise that could be expected. Show them the two designs and ask for their non-binding preference. My anguished inner groans turned to an audible sigh of relief when, without being told which of the two the judges had chosen, they voted by a substantial majority for the maple leaf. Skilful Anthony Mann made the presentation. His theory of choice proved correct. He was my hero.

November 27. Cabinet viewed the stylized maple leaf backed by the board, the minister, and the National Conference, and approved.

We had decided as a policy to allow the symbol to be used on commercial products, and to our surprise opposition came swiftly from Expo '67. On December 11, 1964, Expo's general manager wrote to us:

> There is little doubt that free national use of the emblem of the Commission would entail severe financial losses in the marketing of the emblem of the Exhibition which is the major project of the Centennial celebrations...it would be in our common interest if the Commission would agree not to issue its emblem to commercial concerns but to restrict its distribution to public bodies alone.

Tense meetings were held in Montreal and Ottawa on the issue, Big Brother bullying Poor Cousin, but we held our ground and they eventually backed off, leaving us to exploit this hard-won emblem as we saw fit.

On January 19, 1965, a press conference was held in the Railway Committee Room of the House of Commons and the symbol was launched, twenty-seven days before the flag became official. The three contest winners were sent their money and their names were announced (our untruth about their designs guilefully added to by saying that Stuart Ash had come fourth: Do governments lie?).

That was the day I felt I finally earned a Ph.D. in symbols.

The symbol was registered as a state emblem, a graphics manual was prepared showing how to use it, and a limited number of variations were outlined. The symbol was put into the public domain and advertised in magazines and newspapers. Commercial firms were invited to apply it without charge to products or services. We reasoned that charging for use of the symbol ran counter to the spirit of the Centennial and might have had an inhibiting effect on the maximum currency of its use, that we felt was so desirable.

The wise and canny Georges Gauthier, who had succeeded Robert Choquette, arranged for the collector of customs in major Canadian cities to dispense upon request application forms for permission to use the symbol and to provide copies of the graphics manual containing finished, camera-ready artwork. Thus, the symbol would always appear in the same form. There was no competing Centennial symbol. This was it. Always like this. No variations. The rest is indeed history.

In the succeeding three years, the symbol was to appear on postage stamps, coins from the Royal Canadian Mint, paper money, flags, banners, lapel pins, all federal government cheques, billboards, pamphlets, stationery, every piece of literature in support of every Centennial project and so on. Impressions of the symbol ran into the billions.

In mid-1966 at the urging of the Commission, the Department of Finance began printing the Centennial symbol on every cheque it issued. This practice, which continued right through 1967, may seem rather run-of-the-mill, but the aggregate awareness it created is incalculable. It was impossible to escape the symbol. Month after month, it appeared on child allowance cheques, salary cheques, cheques in payment for goods and services, pension cheques, social security cheques, millions of cheques issued to hundreds of thousands of Canadians.

And on all those Centennial projects of a lasting nature, the symbol was dutifully applied.

The sands of time eroded the nose of the recumbent great Sphinx of Giza, but it is a certainty that many generations of Canadians in the future will be able to see the symbol and read on some edifice in every province in Canada:

Erected with the financial assistance
of
the Government of Canada
In commemoration of the Centennial of Confederation
1967

The Centennial symbol also made a stellar appearance on some 5,500,000 medallions produced by the Royal Canadian Mint at the instigation of the Commission and distributed to primary schoolchildren throughout Canada with the co-operation of the minister of education in each province. The medallion was of red brass alloy — 85 percent copper and 15 percent zinc — and $1\frac{1}{4}$ inches in diameter. Each was sealed in a pliofilm envelope. The Mint selected professional designers and sculptors to participate in a closed competition for a design for the front and obverse.

A symbolic presentation ceremony was held on Parliament Hill in May 1967, Governor General Vanier addressing the youth of the nation and presenting medallions to two students (one boy and one girl) from each province and territory.

The merit of this program was that it gave teachers an opportunity to explain the significance of the Centennial. Here was something tangible to hold onto. Few kids ever get medals. This time, everyone got one.

Did it impress? Probably, because the little ceremony was clothed in dignity, the object had intrinsic value, and it made each kid aware that he or she was part of something pretty important and pretty big. Identity.

The Mint was called upon to produce again, the object this time being the Centennial Medal, awarded to individuals for their service to Canada during the Centennial celebrations. It was silver, with the Queen on the front and on the obverse the royal cipher *EiiR* surmounted by a crown superimposed on a single maple leaf within the inscription *Confederation Canada*. The medal hung from a fine red and white silk ribbon, and was encased in a handsome metal case covered in blue leather and lined in white satin. Calls went out far and wide from the minister's office for recommendations as to who should receive the medals. The government through the secretary of state would accept recommendations only from national and provincial authorities, and from national associations and societies engaged in philanthropic and charitable and scientific activities. Individual applications from members of the public were not considered.

Twenty-seven thousand medals were handed out without ceremony. Perhaps a little homespun to-do in the office after work one day, but nothing grand.

The medal probably appealed to individuals who had never been recognized for anything they had done in life before and would not likely be recognized again. But as a Canadian civilian honour, it has to rank pretty low on the list. Its relative insignificance did not stop some employment seekers after 1967 stating on their résumés, "Recipient of the Centennial Medal." It presaged the whole concept of civilian honours and the institution of the Order of Canada which came along four years later (the Order of Canada rosette is remarkably similar to the twelve-petalled flower that was the second choice for the Centennial symbol).

COINS, CURRENCY AND STAMPS

The Mint's greatest effort went into the design and production of a new issue of coin for 1967. One-cent, five-cent, ten-cent, twenty-five-cent, fifty-cent and the *pièce de résistance*, a twenty-dollar gold coin, containing a half-ounce of twenty-two karat gold. It was produced in a limited edition of 334,000 and handsomely packaged in a way similar to the Centennial Medal. The coin was intended for the numismatic trade and sold well. At the time, gold was pegged worldwide at $35 U.S. per ounce, so the sets retailed for $40. (A premium was charged for the packaging.)

The sets made handsome presentation pieces and were ordered in substantial numbers by senior officers of the Commission to give away to dignitaries and other worthies. At the end of Centennial year one director had twenty sets left in a file drawer and with commendable honesty (if reluctantly), he returned them to the Mint. The price of gold twelve years later had surged to $850 per ounce, giving a market value of at least $500. While said director might have had thoughts of petty larceny in 1967, had he yielded to temptation, petty would have turned to grand the day the price of gold was allowed to float freely in world markets.

Not to be left out, the Bank of Canada produced a one-dollar bill displaying the Centennial symbol, using the plates for the regular one-dollar bill but deleting the serial numbers. So today there are a number of one-dollar bills circulating in the market-place without any numbers. Oddities!

Stamps are, of course, great collector's items, so it is not surprising that the Post Office got into the act. The official five-cent stamp contained all the icons: the flag, the map of Canada, the symbol. In April 1967 came a stamp commemorating Expo '67, on June 30 one marking the royal visit, and in July one for the Pan-Am Games in Winnipeg.

A sense of national identity and pride were enhanced by the medallion, coin and stamp programs. All bore the Centennial symbol, which was a unifying force throughout the celebrations. Whether it appeared on everyday items like cheques or on permanent treasures like medallions and buildings, it was easily recognizable, known to everyone and therefore an element that strengthened the bonds between all Canadians. It belonged to everybody. Everybody used it. And what's more, everybody loved it.

CHAPTER 7

Of Precedents and Planning

T HE ONE-DOLLAR-MATCHING Centennial Grants Program was perhaps the one program that got off the ground with relative ease. While it was being organized in 1963, Robbins Elliott, the director of planning, was wrestling with the challenge of figuring out what the rest of the Centennial celebrations were going to be all about.

He started with the wish list that had emanated from the Centenary Council, and in order to evaluate each item and substantiate its possible inclusion, in June 1963, he established advisory committees. About a dozen of them. They were heavily loaded with academics, many of whom were historians. It was this process that provided him with the assistance he needed to shape the program envisioned in the spare language of the Act.

Canadian precedents were not much help to him. There were only two. The first was the sixtieth anniversary of Confederation in 1927, and the second was the celebration British Columbia staged in 1958 to mark the one-hundredth anniversary of its inauguration as a Crown colony. Canada was at war in 1917 and so did not mark its fiftieth anniversary — apart from issuing a special three-cent postage stamp showing the classic Harris painting of the Fathers of Confederation meeting at Quebec in 1864. The 1927 celebration had more substance.

In proper collegial spirit, although strictly speaking it wasn't my responsibility, I undertook the limited research needed and made a report to Fisher and Elliott. Although I did not recognize it at the time, the 1927 celebrations had met many of the classic criteria for a successful anniversary bash. Reinforcement of identity, reassurance, accentuation of unifying elements, recognition of achievement, a focus on present values and a looking forward.

The Right Honourable George P. Graham was in charge of the National Jubilee Committee and the celebrations were held mostly in Ottawa.

The House of Commons' Peace Tower was completed that year and much was made of its carillon pealing forth at the stroke of noon, playing "O Canada," "The Maple Leaf Forever" and "God Save the King." An 800-voice adult choir backed by the voices of 2,000 children accompanied the bells. The assemblage on the Hill was the largest ever seen, and two first aid units treated 151 persons for heat prostration.

A spectacular parade was mounted, twenty-six floats in all, with every band in Ottawa marching between them as they wound their way through the streets of Ottawa and Hull. *The Ottawa Citizen* described the floats as "symbolizing the growth and marvelous development of the Dominion from the earliest days — a spectacle of historic beauty and splendour." Themes included early European explorers of Canada like Jacques Cartier; Samuel de Champlain; Pierre Gaultier de Varennes et de La Vérendrye; the United Empire Loyalists, refugees of the American Revolution; the fur trade; Arctic discovery; the Royal Canadian Mounted Police; Canadian waterways; the immigration "melting pot"; forestry; wheat; lumbering; and fisheries. The final float, "Confederation," was described as showing Canada seated on a dais with the nine provinces represented by maidens, each bearing the shield of her province. At the head of this float rose a "golden angel of peace and goodwill."

One of the most exciting events of the celebrations would seem to have been the landing of Charles Lindbergh and party by aircraft near the Ottawa Hunt and Golf Club. Six thousand people turned out for the spectacle, which included three planes of the RCAF greeting the party in the air on its approach to Ottawa. Lindbergh was an international hero and the technology of air travel was new. It was a brilliant idea to have him land in Ottawa on July 1, 1927, as a portent of the future. No single event in 1967 was this spectacularly forward-looking.

A radio broadcast from the Hill, transmitted coast to coast on July 1, included the reading of a message from the King, renditions of French Canadian folk songs by one Miss Eva Gauthier and similar English ditties by University of Toronto's Hart House Quartet. There was an official issue of postage stamps and a commemorative medal was struck and given to all schoolchildren. Some Boy Scout troops held little commemorative services at the graves of some of the Fathers of Confederation.

International recognition was slim. The president of the New York Canadian Club presented a tablet to be placed in the House of Commons and Canadian Rotarians who were in convention at Ostend, Belgium, held a Jubilee luncheon. The Duke of Connaught sent a telegram to the "great Dominion whose glorious service to the Empire in the Great War will never be forgotten." Apart from these minor tributes, however, the party stayed within the confines of home.

The *Ottawa Journal* reported that the events in the nation's capital were marred by two occurrences. The first was that a giant seaplane kept circling the Peace Tower during the July 1 ceremonies, drowning out significant portions of the sung and spoken word. The second was that it was suspected that saboteurs (mischief-makers?) had loosened the wheels on some of the floats. When they broke down on the Chaudière Bridge, regular traffic heading into Quebec got into the parade, cut it in two, and by the time the floats were repaired, the viewing throngs in Hull had dispersed, not realizing they had seen only half the parade!

The celebrations all seem rather touching. A young country still strongly tied to Britain, doing its best with modern technology, the populace responding warmly. Canada had yet to go through the Great Depression and World War II and the extensive industrialization that followed. It was still a small, royalist country, much of the English-speaking population patronizing in its attitude toward Quebec. While the celebrations sound somewhat parochial, they were appropriate for their time.

Nothing much was gained from this research except the idea of a medallion for school kids, and the Boy Scouts and the graves of the Fathers. These activities were staged again in 1967. (The Boy Scout tribute got them off the hook. All they had to do was copy the 1927 plans and make it their Centennial project.)

The celebration held in British Columbia in 1958 was more extensive, and a hardcover book had been published, describing what happened then. When a copy of this tome was obtained, Commission staff fell upon it with a glad cry. Here clues would be found. But the British Columbia celebration was regional, provincial, different in kind and in degree to the "sky's the limit" trans-Canada scenario that was to take place in 1967.

We had to conclude that we could get very little help by looking at the Canadian precedents. No effort was made to search the history books to see if any other nation had faced the same challenge we were now facing. Some of us made a pilgrimage to the World's Fair, which was held in New York in 1963, but this was not fruitful. At the Commission we were not planning a World's Fair; we were planning a national celebration.

Elliott's first planning challenge was the date 1964. The two determining preludes to Confederation — the 1864 Charlottetown Conference and the Quebec Conference — called for some kind of commemoration, but the date was drawing closer and nothing was coming to mind. Dr. Frank McKinnon and Maurice Lamontagne had committed to build those Centennial theatres for the two cities, but something more seemed required.

A re-enactment program was hastily organized and staged by Robbins' still embryonic staff in August and September 1964, in the Atlantic provinces and Quebec City. The Fathers were all there, in period costumes, at the places and at the dates where the momentous events had taken place one hundred years before. It required professional stage actors to carry it off and Canada had lots of good ones who were glad of the work. A kind of script was written but the play was really a pageant without props. A difficult show to mount and to carry off convincingly. It could not avoid being stilted, a kind of curiosity, but it was a tribute.

At the time of the re-enactment in Charlottetown, a group of ladies from that city presented a performance of "The Ladies of the Provinces Confederation Parade" in Charlottetown and Saint John. The performance was repeated in several communities in Saskatchewan and Manitoba. The parade was really a Confederation-period fashion show. For the viewers, it satisfied a sort of "local-history-museum" curiosity, but it was weak and not at all national in connotation.

Early in 1964, respected Canadian playwright Tommy Tweed was commissioned to write a Confederation play, which he called *The Dream*, and a touring company performed this to a respectable degree of acclaim in the western provinces in the autumn of 1965.

These two programs were financed totally by the Commission, and the modest publicity that attended the events did help create some awareness of the coming Centennial, but the shows were mere palliatives to relieve the feeling in many quarters that the Commission did not have a handle on the main event!

Apart from Robbins' advisory committee process, there were plenty of suggestions about what to do. Most of these came by mail addressed to "John Fisher, P.O. Box 1967, Ottawa." John was enthusiastically stumping up and down the country, and the publicity he generated for the fact of the upcoming Centennial, elicited "here's what you ought to do" responses from the general public. Others came from opportunists who had an ongoing program that would benefit from augmented funding or whose project was in dire financial straits and who grasped at Centennial funds for rescue. Both of these types tried to put a Centennial spin on their good works in an attempt to make their case. These parties were in the main dealt with by a "no" couched in diplomatic language, the standard phrase being "It doesn't fill a gap at this time in the emerging program."

One exception was an appeal from the publishers of *The Dictionary of Canadian Biography*. This valuable reference work was half-finished and they could not find funds to complete the scholarly work required to complete the entries. It looked like a reasonable request. We gave them several hundred thousand dollars in 1963 and for months when we were chided about having no program, we would sheepishly cite them as an example. Someone yielded to pressure on this one. It was not a true-blue Centennial project. Not at that level of expenditure anyway.

The general public contributed only a few ideas at first, but as awareness grew, these increased in number, in direct proportion to the proximity of Centennial year. A young lad in Alberta believed the Commission should save the wild mustangs that roamed the foothills. Whether they faced extinction or not, whether their survival had a Centennial connotation or not, he persisted in importuning the Commission to "Save the Mustangs." Another enterprising Albertan built a landing pad for a flying saucer and urged the Commission to stage at least one Centennial event at the site in St. Paul, Alberta. And indeed, that is where the helicopter-borne National Conference meeting was later held.

Very few of these early unsolicited proposals were accepted, and as a well-rounded package of programs began to emerge, it was too late to try to accommodate well-intentioned applicants.

By March 1964, after nine months of gestatory verification, the Planning Branch brought forth a basic program. Ideas emanating from the superb plural membership of the CCC were clearly evident in many of the elements.

The program, projects and events of Canada's Centennial year, as they eventually evolved, are described in the following three chapters. They are ordered roughly into groups, the individual components in each group having in common certain of the classic aspects of anniversary. Because some of the components satisfy more than one criterion, this structuring is not a completely accurate reflection of their character. However, by setting them out in this way, it should be easier for organizers of other celebrations to choose events and projects that they would like to emulate.

OF PAGEANTRY AND REASSURANCE

RCMP Musical Ride   Military Tattoo
Folk Festivals   *Voyageur* Canoe Pageant
Native Peoples   Confederation Train
Heads of State Visits   and Caravans
"Son et Lumière" Spectacle

IMPROVEMENT AND FUTURE FOCUS

Tree and Shrub Planting and   Festival Canada
   Community Improvement   Visual Arts Program
Athletic Awards, Fitness   National Gallery
   and Amateur Sports   TV and Film
Publications Program   National Film Board
Interfaith   Art Film Libraries

FUN AND SHARED EXPERIENCE

Bathtub Race   Party on the Hill
Centennial Barge   Alpha and Omega
Centennial Square Dance Train   Youth Travel

These are the broad outlines. Now you can sit back and read about what the anniversary compulsion produced.

Here it comes, folks. One might say, "1967 and all that."

CHAPTER 8

Of Pageantry and Reassurance

AGEANTRY AND POMP ARE A necessary part of any national celebration, and Canada was unstinting in providing large-scale events that showed its citizens their past and present identities in living colour. Some played up well-known Canadian symbols; others reinforced the bonds of the separate communities that make up the country. All brought a sense of ceremony, adventure or fun to the festivities.

RCMP MUSICAL RIDE

The Royal Canadian Mounted Police are not only law enforcers; they also constitute a symbol of Canadian rectitude and strength in the face of danger. Fortunately for the Centennial organizers, this potent symbol also came complete with a ready-made promotional piece — the RCMP Musical Ride. First performed on January 15, 1887, in Regina, the equestrian show was performed sporadically after that until 1961 when it became a permanent fixture, performing in Ottawa and other sites regularly since that date.

In 1967 the Mounties made their first-ever, coast-to-coast tour of Canada. Forty-one officers were involved, including thirty horses and riders who put on the show in an area one hundred feet by two hundred feet, to the accompaniment of music played by the fifty-member RCMP military band. The horses and riders trot, canter and charge, finally paying their respects to the guest of honour at the performance in a ride-past, the horses kneeling in homage at one point. The precision, dexterity and uniformity of the performance never fails to elicit gasps of amazement and appreciation.

Here was a national unifying event involving a Canadian symbol that has deep historical roots. Every performance was sold right out. Visitors leaving the show couldn't help but be proud to be Canadian.

FOLK FESTIVALS

All Canadians, apart from the Indians and Inuit, are immigrants or descendants of immigrants. The so-called "two founding races" — French and English — don't ponder this fact very much, but all the others do. While they are often referred to *sotto voce* as "ethnics" by the descendants of the older immigrants, this is unfair, and because of the quasi-pejorative tone, inexcusable. But it is an easy shorthand and no harm is intended. These newer Canadians have chosen modern Canada as their country. Their varied backgrounds, traditions and cultural expressions contribute to a rich and valuable societal mix.

This richness often remains unnoticed, unappreciated and misunderstood because new immigrants go to the cities, where the work is, and disappear as a group from general view. Their unique cultural expressions are still there, however, and are manifested in music, song, costumes, literature and drama. While the latter two manifestations are difficult to project out into the larger society, the former are not.

Centennial year gave Canada's diverse cultural communities a chance to reflect on their own identities — often through folk art and dance — though in some ways this was unfortunate. The song-and-dance routine is not the most important aspect of the rich diversity which they all bring to Canada. But it is what is at hand, and they use it. More perhaps than other Canadians, they yearned for rituals that validate the past and reinforce identity. The response from Canada's ethnic communities was overwhelming. If *The Anniversary Axiomatique* had been available at the time, the Centennial planners could have cultivated this response and made the experience more fulfilling.

Leon Kossar, executive director of the Canadian Folk Arts Council, was the impresario of this program. He knew his constituency, and they trusted and respected him. His was a significant contribution to cross-cultural appreciation, and to reinforcement of identity.

In every province there was a Canadian Folk Arts Council. Leon Kossar and Stan Kolar from the planning staff of the Commission conceived of the idea of presenting one hundred folk arts festivals during 1967, several in each of the ten provinces, with performers from one province visiting performers of the same ethnic group in other provinces. The visits were timed to coincide with local festivals, thus giving the visiting groups an opportunity to display their talents on the Centennial stage.

The folk arts festivals and cultural exchanges were backed financially by the Centennial Commission and the Centennial authorities in each province. This financial assistance enabled all the folk arts groups to present lively manifestations of their heritage to a far wider audience than their modest resources would otherwise have permitted. Canadians everywhere were thus treated to a remarkable display of cultural knowledge right in their own backyard, presented by fellow Canadians. Once again precious increments of understanding and new appreciation were gained.

Anyone planning to incorporate diverse cultural celebrations into a mega-anniversary should keep these points in mind: encourage different cultural groups to express themselves (far from being a divisive force, this kind of celebration may increase understanding between ethnic communities) and make sure the program director is respected by the cultural groups he or she is working with. This can be a unique opportunity to encourage the evolution of their co-existent integration into the multicultural society.

NATIVE PEOPLES

As it was for Canada's ethnic minorities, so it was for native Canadians. The Centennial was made to order. Just as new Canadians are fiercely proud of their country of choice, native Canadians are fiercely proud of their unique status. The impending one-hundredth anniversary and 1967 itself galvanized many native communities and enhanced native and non-native pride in native cultures.

The first opportunity for reinforcement of community identity came with the announcement of the Centennial Grants Program. Sixty-one Indian reserves across Canada got into the act and built community halls, skating and curling rinks, sports fields, rodeo arenas, art galleries, museums and monuments. The Soowalie band of British Columbia decided to use its grant to restore the early pit dwellings of their ancestors. An interdepartmental Indian Centennial Advisory Committee comprised of representatives of the Citizenship Branch, Indian Affairs Branch and the Centennial Commission reviewed submissions from Indian groups. An Indian Centennial Consultant Committee made up of native leaders from the provinces was formed to identify potential areas for the development of Centennial celebrations and projects and to assess their effectiveness. Sam Cormier and Jean Lagace were two of the staff officers running this program. Sam was an Acadian whose ancestors had been hidden from the British by Micmacs, following the Acadians' expulsion from Nova Scotia, and Jean was a Métis from Winnipeg. Métis is an honourable term. One of mixed parentage. French and Indian.

On the schedule of native events were those that focused on the rich heritage of native customs, legends, stories, songs and dances. These were displayed in pow-wows, potlatches, sports meets, pageants, exhibitions and ceremonials. Dignity and seriousness prevailed when appropriate, but when they had fun, they really had fun — evidence of the phenomenon that Manning describes: that "play predominates in celebrations ... among minorities within modern society where the organizers are in a subordinate position."

Editors of native publications were invited to a conference in Ottawa where they could upgrade their technical skills. A special effort was made to see that teenaged native Canadians were included in the youth travel and athletic programs. The aggregate effect of all this activity funded by the Centennial Commission was to bring native Canadians together as a unified group. While a National Indian Council had been in existence since 1961, the Centennial year activities helped strengthen its members, providing them with increased confidence and hope for self-determination. The macro-organization split into two groups in 1968, the National Indian Brotherhood and the Native Council of Canada, later amalgamating into the powerful and respected Assembly of First Nations of today.

For many of the younger natives, the travel and athletic competitions represented a first experience of the world outside the reserve — and a great boost in self-image. Their pride was also stirred by media reports of native cultural events across Canada. This introduction to the wider native and non-native culture led some to seek more education. Many entered university, a scholastic level heretofore seemingly remote. Some eventually travelled to England to do postgraduate legal work in the field of aboriginal rights. Some, in time, would argue land-claim cases before the courts with passion, eloquence and unique legal knowledge. Ken Goodwill, now a councillor of the Standing Buffalo Band, Fort Qu'appelle, Saskatchewan, was in charge of the "Indian" program. His wife Jean, a registered nurse who graduated at a time when it was rare for native people to pursue professional careers, was admitted as an Officer of the Order of Canada, April 29, 1992. Her citation called her a trail blazer and a role model and an inspiration to young native women. According to Jean, "1967 was the first time government recognized the validity of Indian culture, language and political aspirations in a substantial way. In gaining this recognition they were encouraged and supported financially by the Centennial Commission. Things would never be the same again."

Ever since the arrival of the Europeans, Canada's native peoples had been viewed as socially and culturally inferior.

Centennial year did much to improve their self-esteem and enhance their status in the eyes of other Canadians.

VISITS FROM HEADS OF STATE

While a mega-anniversary involves fun, remembrance, reassurance and the giving of gifts, another aspect is required to make it complete, and that is dignity. The great nineteenth-century political philosopher Walter Bagehot wrote that the monarchy provides for the dignified aspects of the Constitution. The constitution of anniversaries calls for its dignified aspect as well.

The parish priest, the pastor or the rabbi is invited to a fiftieth wedding anniversary. To corporate anniversaries you invite the heads of other corporations not only because you want them to share in the celebration, but because their presence adds lustre and dignity, raising the whole affair up a notch. In 1967 Canada's Centennial festivities were raised up a notch by means of formal visits from heads of state of all the nations exhibiting at Expo '67. Ninety-two accepted.

Normally visits from heads of state are handled by a unit in the office of the secretary of state. In 1967 a special office, the Official Visits Office, was established to undertake the extra tasks arising from the vast numbers of visits from dignitaries. The office was headed by The Honourable Lionel Chevrier, ex-Liberal Cabinet minister.

As you can't properly receive two heads of state on the same day, one of his tasks was to juggle the availability of all these dignitaries and to smooth out potential scheduling conflicts. The routine was this: after visiting Expo, the head of state travelled to Ottawa for a formal reception. The Centennial Commission had nothing to do with these arrangements, although Judy LaMarsh as secretary of state received them all when they came to Ottawa.

One head of state had unique standing, and warranted extra-special treatment and an extra-long visit. Her Majesty, Elizabeth the Second, Queen of Canada, and of course, he who walks one pace behind, her consort, the Duke of Edinburgh.

Canada is a monarchy. Whether this fact is viewed as a vestige of colonial status, an anachronism in the modern age, a contradiction of self-determination, a blessing for which we sing to God to save, or a structural institution that we would have to invent if we hadn't inherited it ready-made, it remains a fact. Everything in government in Canada is done in the name of the Queen. Every law of the Parliament of Canada and each of the provincial legislatures contains a preamble reminding us of this, and every bit of new legislation is a dead letter unless and until it is proclaimed into law by the representative of the Queen — either the governor general of Canada or a lieutenant-governor of the subject province. Royalist feelings still run deep in the hearts of many Canadians, even though our Constitution has been completely repatriated and has nothing to do with England. Other Canadians, including many Québécois, view the monarchy as an outdated concept. In their view, it is incongruous and anachronistic to be subject to a ruler who is a citizen and resident of a foreign country.

Traditionally, Québécois have been respectful of authority figures. They respected their new titular head of state following their conquest by the British, and the conditioning of the Church only reinforced their deference to those who held power. In the past, Quebec parishioners rarely questioned the teachings of the parish priest, who was authority personified. But this has changed since the Quiet Revolution. It's a safe bet that many more people in Quebec would vote no to the Queen than in the rest of Canada. But we aren't a republic yet. And if we were, we'd have to invent a Queen figure. The dignified aspect is essential.

We wanted the Queen in Canada in 1967. We wanted her on July 1 in Ottawa on the very birthday, as many thought of it, and she came. A five-day royal visit.

It was pleasant enough. Everyone went ga-ga and it rained only once. Unlike her command visit in 1964 to Quebec City when separatist tensions were so strong that she had to be hustled from A to B surrounded by a phalanx of police and guards, the fear of assassination was minimal.

She, who provides the dignified aspects of state, performed with dignity. A mysterious function. A necessary function. A very good person in that office, she provided for the quintessence of what is innately longed for at a time of anniversary celebration. Continuity, assurance, reassurance, comfort. God Save the Queen.

Another head of state who accepted Canada's invitation to come visit us in 1967 was General Charles André Joseph Marie de Gaulle, warrior, political leader, patriot, statesman, president of the French Fifth Republic and author of three books: *The Call to Honour, Unity* and *Salvation.* The politicians in Quebec City were ecstatic to have *le grand Charles* in their midst. Here was the epitome of French language and culture, of French survivance, a living legend, all six-foot-five of him.

They scrubbed Highway 40, the Trans-Canada Highway, from Quebec City to Montreal, and painted *fleur de lys* down the centre line — all one hundred and fifty-six miles of it — so that as his cavalcade rolled into Expo he would be conscious that he was on family soil. Once again, one observes the quintessence of celebration: continuity, assurance, reassurance, comfort. But this time in French.

He who had written *Call to Honour, Unity,* and *Salvation* got carried away, and in four words, "Vive le Québec libre" (Long live a free Quebec), simultaneously received thunderous acclaim from the throng in front of Montreal's City Hall and disturbed and angered most of Canada, eliciting a rebuke from a shocked Prime Minister Pearson.

"Unacceptable," said Pearson.

Plans for the formal reception in Ottawa were scrubbed and de Gaulle was sent packing, back to his beloved France with an open day in his crowded calendar. It was sad. Was he just insensitive, or did he mean it? Either way, given the circumstances, he harmed the cause of unity in Canada at the very height of a year of pan-Canadian solidarity and family fun.

SON ET LUMIÈRE

In its quest for grand spectacles, the Centennial Commission sent researchers to Europe to investigate a type of historical pageantry known as "Son et Lumière." These large-scale presentations use historic buildings as backdrops for sound-and-light shows depicting important events in history.

When the researchers returned, they put together a team to stage a similar kind of show in front of the Parliament Buildings in Ottawa. Viewed from an eight-hundred-seat amphitheatre at Nepean Point Park adjacent to the Parliament Buildings, two productions were held during the summer of 1967, dramatizing historic events known to have occurred in and around Parliament. As in any sound-and-light show, there were no visible actors. Only mono, stereo and travelling sound, plus floodlights, music and voices. Well-known Canadian actors Bud Knapp, Kate Reid and Mavor Moore were among those doing a voice gig. The music was by Neil Chotem.

The gothic Parliament Buildings were an ideal backdrop, and the Ottawa River flowing behind it added depth to the episodes about explorers like Samuel de Champlain, who actually used that waterway to make their way into unmapped territories. However, the show was confusing at times, which made it difficult to keep the audience's interest. A commendable initiative in projecting Canada's history onto the "big screen," but not a great success.

In spite of the expensive investment in infrastructure, the show was scrubbed in the autumn of 1967 and did not see the light of day again. "Son et Lumière" is a European concept and had never been tried in Canada before. To amortize the cost of the infrastructure, it really needs to operate twelve months of the year, and Canada's harsh winter makes this impossible.

MILITARY TATTOO

At the suggestion of the Centennial Commission, Canada's Armed Forces staged a Centennial military tattoo. An outdoor entertainment given at night, consisting of military exercises accompanied by music, the tattoo idea originally developed in

Europe. Apart from making the initial suggestion, the Commission was not involved in this production. But they did not need to be. The military did a superb job on their own.

From March to October 1967, the Department of National Defence staged the tattoo in forty communities coast to coast. The travelling spectacular portrayed three hundred years of Canada's military history. There were bands, acrobatics, displays of precision drill and motorcycles leaping through rings of fire.

The tattoo met many of the requirements of a successful anniversary celebration. It dramatized Canadian exploits in the two world wars, thus reinforcing identity and offering reassurance about Canada's value as a player on the world stage. The spectacle was dignified in parts but also had its share of clowns on motorcycles and other fun acts.

While Canadians were enjoying the tattoo, some members of the military were left out of the Centennial celebrations. Armed Forces personnel stationed in Europe, Africa, Pakistan, India and Cyprus were nevertheless given a chance to be part of the festivities as "Variety '67," a Canadian Forces variety show, brought the Centennial to the military-in-exile. All part of reaffirming national identity — a key component of anniversary celebrations.

VOYAGEUR CANOE PAGEANT

Along with the Mountie and the beaver, the canoe is one of Canada's most recognizable symbols. Used by the Hudson's Bay Company and the *voyageurs* of the North West Company in the fur trade, canoes embody the Canadian spirit of wilderness adventure and they had much to do with opening the country up for settlement. Many of Canada's European explorers were employees of one fur-trading company or the other.

When Canadian kids go off to summer camp they are taught how to handle a canoe. Powerboats and sailboats may be moored at the docks of summer cottages across Canada, but there is almost always a canoe there too, lying upside down on the dock with two paddles underneath. They are usually made of fibreglass or aluminum now, instead of birchbark, but a canoe is a canoe, and a paddle is a paddle, and no Canadian celebration would be complete without canoes.

That is why the concept of a canoe race from the west coast to the east coast began to take shape in the minds of the Centennial planners. They wanted to pay a tribute to the courage, vision and stamina of the founders of Canada.

The idea of a race was abandoned because it became clear that some paddlers would be faster than others, and if a few canoes consistently outstripped the others, an opportunity would be lost to capitalize on the colourful assembly of canoes and canoeists. So the planners settled on a pageant.

The pageant was elaborate and spectacular. Canoeists from all the provinces and territories were invited by the Centennial Commission to paddle a brigade of canoes from Rocky Mountain House in Alberta to Montreal, a distance of 3,283 miles, during the period from May 24 to September 4. There is no canoe tradition in the two island provinces, Prince Edward Island and Newfoundland, and hence no canoeists, so these provinces did not participate. But nine provinces and the Yukon Territory fielded crews.

A Canoe Pageant Division headed by W.H.A. Mathews was established and staffed principally with staff skilled in logistics. The ninety paddlers came from the three oceans that touch Canada's shores and the lands between. Among them were loggers, miners, farmers, guides, trappers, musicians, railroaders, native chiefs, Inuit hunters, school principals, labourers, professional skiers and paddlers. The average age was about twenty-five, the youngest being seventeen and the oldest fifty-one. Each team was made up of tough competitors, but they were a colourful lot with high spirits when the day's work was done. Around the campfires at night, fiddlers, bagpipers, guitarists, drummers, folk singers, step dancers and jig and reel artists brought early Canadian songs and dances back to life.

The canoes were built on the model of the *voyageurs'* north canoes — the ones they used to travel from Lake Superior to the farthest points north. They were 25 feet long, 4 feet wide, and 18 inches deep, weighed about 260 pounds and were painted to look like birchbark. Each canoe carried the name of the province or territory it represented and the name of an explorer it was honouring. All were made in St. Jean des Piles, Quebec.

In 1965 and 1966, trials were held to test men, equipment, methods and administration. In 1965, a team took a run from North Bay, Ontario, through Georgian Bay to Kingston, through the Trent Canal and Lake Ontario. In 1966, a western trial of 600 miles saw all teams run the Fraser River in British Columbia, starting at Prince George in the interior and travelling through to Victoria on Vancouver Island. A 450-mile eastern trial took the paddlers from Lac St. Jean, Quebec, past Montreal, through Lake Champlain and the Hudson River to New York City.

For anyone interested in organizing a canoe pageant, the following are some helpful details about the organization of the pageant that was actually staged in 1967. Four methods of water travel were used. The first was the lap. There were thirty-four of these, which meant a timed start and finish, and paddlers racing all day for distances up to seventy-five miles. The second was the brigade, in which the teams started out together and were timed but did not race. They were paced to arrive together in a community, where they put on a display of their skill. The third method was the sprint, which was a short timed race from one to five miles staged in communities for the benefit of spectators. The final mode was called the transit, in which paddlers took it easy, stopping for swims or lunch, the only stipulation being that they had to arrive at a specific point at a specific time.

Winning teams paddled sixty strokes a minute or better during long laps. In short sprints, strokes exceeded seventy a minute. In the brigade or transit, they usually paddled at a count of forty per minute. On long runs, speeds of up to seven miles per hour were maintained at a steady pace of ten to fourteen hours a stretch. They did not stop for meals but drank "liquid food" from prepared containers through plastic tubes while paddling. At night the teams slept out in their own tents flying their provincial flags. Unless they were paddling through the wilderness, the brigade would always intersect with a road party that provided logistical support, shopping, laundry, mail and supplies to carry them to the next camp.

All water movement was timed, and the times were added up to determine the overall winner. The team with the shortest travel time from the start to the finish line at Expo '67 in Montreal would win. When all the counts were in, it was clear that the winning team was Manitoba.

Where rapids or other dangerous conditions made paddling impossible, the teams lugged canoes and baggage along portage paths. There were seventy portages altogether, a total of sixty miles. The paddlers walked the whole way, carrying their loads with no outside help. Sometimes the speed on these portages exceeded four miles per hour.

The pageant stopped at ninety communities along its route, where the canoeists were entertained by stampedes, street dancing and balls, goose- and moose-calling contests, fiddling and step dance contests, parades, bands and choirs. And there were feasts of every description: pit-roasted steer, buffalo and moose, barbecues, steamed and smoked fish, pork, sheep and venison specialties.

There was something noble and grand about the canoe pageant as revealed in the map of the final route that appears in the third set of photos in this book. It was noble in the sense that it was a heroic feat to make a journey of that scale by canoe; grand because it was pure Canada.

It also served as a reminder that it is individuals who make up a nation. The aggregate is an abstraction. The individual is specific. The ninety canoe pageant paddlers were individuals who did something to make Canadians feel proud. That pride was evident on September 4 when the brigade of colourful canoes paddled up to the dock at LeHavre at Expo '67, in the brilliant late summer sunshine, to receive the accolades of the secretary of state and assembled well-wishers. They had come a long way. And the towering cityscape of Montreal in the background provided a sobering juxtaposition. It was a brilliant reminder of how far Canada had come since the days of the *voyageurs*.

CONFEDERATION TRAIN AND CARAVANS

Of all Canadian symbols, trains best represent national unity. Without the transcontinental railway, Canada would never have extended from the Atlantic to the Pacific coast. British Columbia agreed to enter Confederation in 1871 only on condition that the rail line be extended across the Rockies to reach the west coast by 1881. If the line had not been completed, British Columbia and the western territories of British North America would possibly have been taken over by the expanding United States. The railroad is therefore a tangible symbol of how Canada first came together.

The main line from Montreal to Vancouver was not actually completed until November 7, 1885, but when it was finally built, the Canadian Pacific Railway was one of the longest railways in the world. Its completion was a monumental engineering feat and a triumph over both financial and geographic obstacles.

In negotiations with the government, and as an incentive to undertake construction, Canadian Pacific initially received a land grant of 25 million acres in lieu of cash to do the job. As much of this land bordered the right of way, the CPR exploited the land's natural resources over the years and branched into operations in mining, forest products, fertilizer, oil and gas.

The railway itself allowed freight and passenger traffic to flow from east to west and back, playing a major role in opening up western Canada and allowing for Canada's economic development.

It is impossible to overemphasize the symbolic significance of the ribbon of steel that ties the country together. The Confederation train capitalized on this powerful symbol and became a successful rolling Centennial project. It was the perfect Canadian anniversary spectacle. For one thing, it was a road show — an excellent means of making a big splash and getting people involved. Furthermore, the road the show travelled on was the national railroad. The concept of a Confederation train was historically meaningful, symbolically accurate, and practical, and it was an efficient and effective means of making the Centennial of Confederation accessible to a large number of Canadians.

The project was conceived by Robbins Elliott and his staff in 1963, early in the Centennial planning process. Les Maiden, formerly a major in the Army's service corps, was put in charge, as chief of the Train and Caravan Division within the Planning Branch. Although it made a lot of sense to use the railway, a problem arose from the fact that the steel rails ran only between the major cities. We would have to find some way to take the show off the rails and send it on the highways and byways to the hundreds of places not serviced by trains. But how were we going to do that? Elliott and Company realized there was only one way.

By truck.

Thus, the concept of the Confederation caravans was born.

Not one caravan. Eight of them.

The itinerary of the Confederation train, which travelled the continent between January 9 and December 5, 1967, reads like an old railway timetable (see Appendix F). The route taken by the eight caravans, the first of which opened on May 1 and the last of which closed on November 1, is included as Appendix G. The detailed plan of the journeys of the Confederation train and the eight Confederation caravans taken together is an atlas of Canada, a "where-the-people-live" atlas, a picture of the country suggested by place names.

In all kinds of weather, $2\frac{1}{2}$ million proud Canadians in 63 communities, lined up to tramp through the Confederation train, and $6\frac{1}{4}$ million eager citizens from 655 other places came to see the caravans. This was about the number expected and the printed material given to each visitor had been ordered in these quantities.

The train consisted of fifteen specially decorated units, of which six were exhibit cars. The Centennial symbol was painted four feet high on the front of the engines and the words

"Canada" and "Confederation" and the dates 1867-1967 were displayed prominently throughout. The familiar wailing blast of the train's whistle was programmed to play the first four notes of "O Canada."

Each caravan consisted of eight 73-foot tractor-trailer units. At each stop, they were set up in a quadrangle. Inside the quadrangle a stage was set up, along with a structure for displaying regional exhibits. The decoration of the units and the detailed design, construction, installation and maintenance of the exhibits were all carried out by the Canadian Government Exhibition Commission, which was established in 1927 as a part of the Department of Trade and Commerce.

In the sixties, exhibit design was in an evolutionary state, moving from purely static form to one containing movement, auditory stimulus and things that could be touched and even smelled. This type of exhibit was used by General Electric at the World's Fair in New York in 1964 and later employed by the Disney Corporation in its theme parks. Exhibits that appealed to all the senses were also incorporated into the design of the Ontario Science Centre in Toronto, the Confederation memorial project of the province of Ontario.

The "story line" for the Confederation train was developed by Blair Fraser and Laurier LaPierre. Journalists, broadcasters and authors, they were chosen to sketch out the story, to help prepare the written text, and put together a sound track in French and English.

Access was controlled so that people had time to linger once they got inside. This, of course, resulted in long lineups, but lining up was accepted as part of the experience. People didn't mind. After all, the caravan comes to us, doesn't it? It's a privilege. Glad to wait. While they stood in line, visitors could glance over a brightly illustrated "keeper piece," a glossy pamphlet that was apparently treasured by all. None were to be found littering the station platform, the shopping malls and the village squares that the train and caravan visited.

Because the Confederation train and the Confederation caravans were the single most expensive project of the Centennial

Commission, and because the content was unique and so specific to the Centennial, it is instructive to read from the keeper piece which described the experience. The document reflected many of the characteristics of good anniversary publications, reinforcing identity and reminding Canadians of their history. It detailed aspects of Canadian society to be proud of: the peaceful birth of the country, our participation in the two world wars, and our openness to immigration. (The piece is reproduced in full in Appendix H.)

The travelling road shows were a looking-back and looking-forward experience. Identity and confirmation were present. So was reassurance. Psychic needs were thus satisfied. It was a celebration of continuity. A fitting response to the anniversary compulsion.

CHAPTER 9

Improvement and Future Focus

R OD CLACK, AN ARCHITECT FROM Victoria, B.C., one of Elliott's stalwarts, devised two programs in his position as a project officer in the Ceremonial Division that fed into the anniversary desire to improve, to look ahead, to do things for future benefit. A kind of metaphor for the New Year's resolution: a resolve to improve, to make things better.

One was a tree and shrub planting program for primary and secondary schools that began in the 1965 spring planting season and continued right through to the 1967 fall season. Some 68,000 instructional brochures were printed and shipped, along with 500,000 plastic tree markers (bearing the symbol, of course), and over a million trees and shrubs were distributed by provincial departments of forestry. The psychology of planting trees is that beyond being just an improvement, a tree is a lasting, growing memorial to an occasion. Young trees are relatively inexpensive, easily distributed, and mass plantings permit mass participation — all of which makes tree planting a superb anniversary activity. In an age of global warming, this kind of celebration also has a helpful environmental side-effect.

The other Clack initiative was a Community Improvement Program consisting of national seminars and the publication of bilingual instruction manuals and filmstrips to make Canadians more aware of their environment and to increase interest in improvement and beautification of individual homes and of whole communities. This compulsion to aggressively clean up, paint up and beautify seems to run with events like a visit from the in-laws or, at a higher level, a special event like a party or an anniversary. Things should look as nice as possible.

In 1934 the city of Toronto fell prey to this compulsion as it celebrated its Centennial. The city encouraged all the public schools to mount campaigns to clean up the community. A questionnaire-like form was distributed to each pupil, with space to tell how many trees had been planted, how many flowers had been planted, how many fences had been painted, etc. One of the boxes called for how many rats had been killed.

My brother and I felt the "rats killed" box was so ludicrous that in our own ludic burst, we each entered 1,934 in the "rats killed" box. We were actually called to a ceremony at City Hall and each presented with a little plaque as an award for killing the most rats in Toronto's Centennial year!

As an architect Rod Clack was a practitioner of one of the fine arts. He was an aesthete, and his aesthetic sense was brought to bear on the urbanscapes and the landscape of Canada. The individual improvements effected were relatively minor, but in aggregate, they made a significant contribution — and many of the trees are still growing.

ATHLETIC AWARDS, FITNESS AND AMATEUR SPORTS

The Centennial Athletic Awards Program was part of a complete athletics program designed and run by the Athletics Division under Roy Boucher within the Planning Branch of the Commission. Details of the program were developed jointly by the Commission and the Canadian Association for Health, Physical Education and Recreation (CAHPER), the Canadian Amateur Speed Skating Association, the Canadian Amateur Swimming Association and the Boy Scouts and Girl Guides of

Canada. The program was administered in co-operation with provincial educational authorities, and a similar program was worked out with the Canadian Association for Retarded Children.

Standards were established in three compulsory and three optional events: the standing broad jump, one-minute speed sit-ups and a three-hundred-yard run. Running, swimming and skating made up the optional tests. Gold, silver and bronze crests and Red Shields were awarded to the $5\frac{1}{2}$ million students aged six to eight who participated.

The athletics program had several other strong components, starting with a university Olympiad in March, in which national university championships were held in hockey, basketball, skiing, judo, swimming and curling, with seven hundred Canadian university students competing at two campuses in Alberta. The first-ever Canadian Winter Games were held in Quebec City in February, with participants from all the provinces. In late July and early August the fifth Pan-American Games, the largest sporting event ever held in North America, was staged in Winnipeg, with 2,500 athletes from 33 countries in competition. Organizers of all these sporting events applied for and received major funding from the Commission.

The Fitness and Amateur Sports Directorate of the Department of National Health and Welfare picked up the Centennial baton with enthusiasm and co-ordinated the efforts of about thirty sports governing bodies that invited countries to come to Canada to compete in specific events. Over one hundred national and international events were staged, some of them world championships, ranging from the Snowshoe Championship in Ottawa in January 1967 to the Canadian Lacrosse Association World Championship in Toronto in May — two events that were very Canadian in flavour. (Lacrosse was invented by the Algonquian tribes of eastern Canada and snowshoes were used by most aboriginal peoples — as a means of walking through deep snow, rather than for sport.) In June, the First Canadian Para-lympic Games were held in Montreal. The gentle Canadian Lawn Bowling World

Invitational Tournament took place in August in the same city, and the down-home Canadian Horseshoe Association World Championship in Toronto in August. Although horseshoes are rarer than they used to be, the metal cleats nailed to the hooves of horses can also be used in the game of horseshoes. The point is to throw the horseshoe so it lands as near as possible to a short stake that has been driven into the ground several metres away.

The organizers of many of these events approached the Commission for financial assistance, and the officers in the Athletics Division dealt with each on its merits, a modest cap being put on how much each could expect by way of subvention. The staging of activities with a Centennial spin was after all the *raison d'être* of the Commission, so we were, rightly, expected to help.

Three exotic athletic events held during Centennial year could not have taken place without Commission support. The first was the Alpine Centennial Expedition in the Yukon, where the Alpine Club of Canada selected ten peaks in the St. Elias Mountains to be scaled by mountaineers from the ten provinces. They also invited an international team to scale a 15,700-foot peak on the Alaska-Yukon border. It was a Centenary in Alaska too: one hundred years had passed since the United States had purchased Alaska from Russia.

A balloon race out of Calgary was staged in the summer of 1967, and this was the first time these colourful behemoths had been seen in Canada. Twelve propane-fired hot-air balloons competed to see how far east of the city they could get, riding the air currents coming down from the Rocky Mountains. (All did succeed in landing safely, east of the city.) The Canadian Camping Association was given a grant to prepare maps of the water routes followed by the early explorers, showing rapids, portages, campsites and Indian lore of the territory. The *coureurs de bois, voyageurs* and other traders and explorers canoed along water routes or tramped through the forest seeking beaver pelts to be shipped back to England to make top hats for the British male gentry. In the early days, there were no trains, no roads, no airports: just water — some rapid, some still — and forest trails, first opened in prehistory by the aboriginal peoples of what is now North America.

The canoe route mapped out by the Canadian Camping Association bore the aura of the aboriginals, the explorers and their exploits, and in giving accuracy and new currency to this retrospective aspect of pure Canadian history, the Camping Association hit upon a crucial aspect of anniversary: looking back and seeing from whence we came. Learning how strong we were and how strong the country made us.

The Centennial Folk Festival and Highland Games were held in Halifax in August. Among other ethnic groups, the Scottish community has had an important effect on Canada's development. Scotland had no overseas empire, but in the nineteenth century, Canada came close to being a Scottish colony. Most of the Hudson's Bay Company traders were Scots: Manitoba's Red River settlement was founded by a Scottish aristocrat, Pictou County in Nova Scotia was settled largely by Scottish crofters and many of the country's banks and universities (including McGill and Queen's) were founded by Scots. Scottish traditions are perhaps best preserved in Nova Scotia, so it is appropriate that the Highland Games were held in that venue.

In the context of mega-anniversary, the psychology appears to have been "It's a special year, so let's do something special." Athletic and sports activities are ubiquitous in our society and some of the events would probably have taken place without the impetus of Centennial. But the fact is that many of them would not have been organized had it not been for the energy and enthusiasm that are part of an anniversary year — to say nothing of the funding made available to underwrite the events.

Athletic programs on a national and local scale are a must for most mega-anniversaries because they embody so many of the axioms that make an anniversary celebration work. Athletic competitions are public performances and they are participatory. They can be unifying if they are staged in a way that brings out healthy rivalry without generating hostility. They are fun —

and they generate pride and a future focus, a desire to achieve even more next time, to stretch beyond apparent limits.

PUBLICATIONS PROGRAM

Athletics exercise the body; books exercise the mind. The Centennial Commission catered to both these needs. General discussion among members of the Commission led to the development of a publications program. André LeBlanc, a former high school teacher, ran this as one of his responsibilities as assistant director of the Planning Branch.

The first component of the program was a mass purchase of books, to be given to libraries across the country. The Commission set itself a budget that allowed it to purchase approximately $130,000 worth of books at retail value. The funds were distributed on a per capita basis on the understanding that the minimum allocated to each province and territory would not fall below $5,000. Centennial authorities in each province and territory selected libraries eligible to receive books as gifts. The libraries, in turn, made a choice of books from the lists established by the Committee up to the amount allocated to each library, according to the following principles:

- 50 percent minimum of the books chosen had to have basic Canadian subject matter;
- at least 20 percent of the budget had to be spent on books printed in French.

This last stipulation was a step in the right direction — a move to bring the French-English equation into balance.

The Commission received proposals from two broad industry organizations — the Co-operative Book Centre of Canada Ltd. and the Conseil Supérieur du Livre — regarding which books to purchase and these two agencies performed all the necessary administrative work. The Co-op Book Centre guaranteed a discount of 34 percent; the Conseil Supérieur a discount of 40 percent. Distribution of the gifts was undertaken by the Queen's Printer.

With a token pile of books on hand, presentation ceremonies were held on July 19, 1967, in all provincial and territorial capitals to mark the gift of 23,000 books about Canada to 451 libraries across the country.

Nationwide and intellectually stimulating, the program was a Centennial shot in the arm to Canada's perennially struggling book publishing industry. It also helped bolster Canadian culture in a country looking for its own voice and heavily influenced by American culture. At a more basic level, books have a lot to do with shaping identity — both personal and national — as they make us look into the past and forward to the future. They are in some sense a memorial, and they can also be used as gifts.

As part of the publications program, ninety-five grants were made to authors and associations to assist in the publication of works on Canadian subjects. Of 850 requests, 103 were recommended, for a total of $262,400. The average grant was $2,550, it being stipulated that no grant would exceed $5,000. Some of the results:

Kaye, V.J., *Dictionary of Ukrainian-Canadian Biography*
McKenty, L., *Political Biography of Mitchell Hepburn*
De Grandpré, P., *Histoire de la littérature canadienne-française*
Beddoe, Allan, *Canadian Heraldry*
Fraser, F., *Blackfoot Indian Tribal Legendary*

Some of these books may have been printed even without the Centennial grants, but some would not likely have seen the light of day. Canadians would then have been the poorer.

As valuable as these many books were, none were linked closely with the Centennial celebrations themselves. Lorraine Monk, chief of the Still Photography Division of the National Film Board, did come up with the idea of a book of photographs of Canadian landscapes to be funded entirely by the NFB. The result was a magnificent coffee table book, *Canada: A Year of the Land.*

INTERFAITH

Religious concerns do not necessarily have to figure into the celebration of an anniversary, but Canada's Centennial Commission did subsidize the activities of the Canadian Interfaith Conference as a way of encouraging unity among the country's different faith communities. The Conference set up a secretariat headed by Rabbi Lavy M. Becker, developed a religious declaration, compiled a bilingual anthology of prayer, created a Centennial anthem and a Centennial hymn, and published and distributed nineteen thousand kits containing all these things. Every minister of every faith community in Canada was contacted and provided with the material. Three large interfaith conferences were also held.

The composer of the Centennial hymn was Rex LeLacheur of the Rex LeLacheur Singers, the lyrics being supplied by Rev. Kenneth Moyer. The three verses, each a quatrain, were respectful and appropriate but did not make the lexicon of enduring Canadian sacred music. The anthem composed by the renowned organist Dr. Healey Willan had lyrics by Robert Choquette. It had five verses, six lines each. The Prince of Poets did a magnificent job: soaring and sensitive, the words deserved to live and could be revived with pride any year, any century.

It is impossible to measure the success of these efforts in creating greater harmony between Canada's religious institutions. However, it is certain that religion allows individuals to reinforce identity, look back, look forward, improve, and have fun — all phenomena that also occur at mega-anniversary time. And since a country's identity is determined partly by its religious beliefs, it was fitting that a religious component be part of the Commission's program.

A Centennial choir of 250 voices recruited from local choral societies and church choirs in the National Capital Region and directed by Nicholas Goldschmidt performed at ceremonies and spectacles on Parliament Hill and at Sunday Service closing Centennial year. Their broad repertoire included the Centennial hymn and anthem.

FESTIVAL CANADA

One of the Centennial's biggest artistic splashes was Festival Canada. From January to December 1967, this ongoing event brought locally, nationally and internationally known talent to all Canadians. It had four components: a touring component, performances by performing arts companies on their home turf, a special program in the National Capital area, and some specific grants and commissions for the creation of new works.

The arts in Canada, as elsewhere, seldom turn a profit at the box office. Someone has to provide the funds to keep them going. While the private sector has often been generous, the main source of funding is usually government. In 1967, it was the Centennial Commission that underwrote the extraordinary expense of Festival Canada — the second-largest line item in the Commission's budget. To run this show the Festival Canada Agency was created, directed by Henry Wrong, an impresario who had worked extensively in Great Britain.

The impresario's role is to manage public entertainment. Normally an impresario represents several artists or artistic groups or, if he is associated with a hall, he books groups, artists or acts into the hall. Henry Wrong did this — but on a much larger scale than normal. His task was to organize and book 12 groups in 98 halls over a period of 12 months. A total of 248 performances all told. The list of groups appears in Appendix E and reveals the scope of the Festival, its variety, and eclectic nature.

Festival Canada permitted many professional companies to display their excellence in many centres in Canada otherwise unable to afford them.

The National Ballet in Rimouski? The Stratford Shakespearean Festival in Fredericton? The Centennial year offered a unique opportunity. Let Canadians everywhere see the best professionals in the performing arts — to enjoy them and be proud of them.

Noteworthy in all of this was the contribution of Quebec, and Festival Canada's performances within Quebec. Among the Quebec tour companies were: Le Théâtre du Nouveau Monde,

Montreal's famous repertory company; Le Théâtre du Rideau Vert, Canada's oldest permanent theatre company; and Les Feux Follets, the National Folk Dance Company headquartered in Montreal. Festival Canada on Tour played twenty cities in Quebec, the majority of the performances given by the three Quebec companies, but these companies moved across Canada as well, and the Les Feux Follets did a national tour.

The Agency operated semi-autonomously, with a Program Development Committee giving direction. Georges Gauthier was chairman. The staff was represented by Robbins Elliott, Claude Gauthier, and Nicholas Goldschmidt, who was chief of the Performing Arts Division of the Commission. (Goldschmidt, a distinguished conductor, had been the first director, inspiration for and impresario of the Vancouver International Festival in the late fifties.) He also organized and conducted the Centennial choir, which was made up of choristers from the National Capital Region. A performer himself, he had good judgement and plenty of energy — an excellent choice to represent the Commission's interests. There were ten other members on the Program Development Committee, the secretary of state and a veritable Who's Who from Expo '67, the Canada Council, the CBC and the Canadian performing arts establishment.

A second component of Festival Canada was Festival Canada at Home. Many professional and some amateur companies — including opera companies, symphony orchestras and theatre companies — presented special Centennial performances in their own local areas. The groups themselves were typical high-quality candidates for Canada Council subsidies; the substance of their performances was not very Centennial.

The Canadian Music Centre, the Canadian Theatre Centre and a university Centennial theatre program all received grants. They were a stimulus. No doubt a rationale could be found.

A real shot in the arm came with the commissioning of works from forty-one Canadian composers to be premièred during 1967. However, the works were hardly "Centennial" in nature. Typical were a concerto· for accordion and chamber orchestration performed by University of Toronto's Hart House Orchestra and the *Sonata for Violin and Piano No. 3*, called *Ballad of the North*, by the Raiston-Moore Duo, Edmonton. If a deadline, some money and encouragement can lead to new musical creation, then there it was. The corpus of Canadian music was enlarged — a landmark contribution to the arts in Canada, since original Canadian classical works have always been scarce.

Two Centennial plays were also commissioned by Festival Canada: one in English, one in French. The English one was a collaborative effort by Canadian novelists Robertson Davies, W.O. Mitchell and Arthur L. Murphy, satirist Eric Nicol and Quebec novelist Yves Thériault. It was an impressive lineup, but like the committee designing the horse, they produced a malformation. The play opened in Ottawa on January 8, 1967, and closed three days later. Talk about not having legs. It didn't have anything. It was awful. Festival Canada deserved something better.

If anything about the program could be criticized, it is the fact that it was weak in popular entertainment. The whole thing was really quite highbrow. John Fisher kept hammering away to have popular aspects included and did succeed in getting engagements for Don Messer and the Islanders, a popular country band from Prince Edward Island, but beyond that there was not much to please the common crowd or young Canadians. This turn of events was hardly surprising, since the anti-popular bias was built right into Festival Canada's promotional literature:

> The word "popular" can mean different things to different people. What is popular in the Atlantic Provinces might not be so in British Columbia. On the other hand what was popular in 1966 might be of no interest in 1967. Therefore, this program as it is planned at the time of writing must remain flexible and should in no way be considered final.

This was a reasonable disclaimer but it really only served to avoid the issue. No risks were taken in the direction of popular cultural events. "Flexible" was never invoked. Festival Canada was consistent and pretty classic.

Festival Canada did have the clout to book the Beatles in 1966 to come to Canada for the Centennial. This is not to say that it was ever considered, but had it been, as the disclaimer stated, would they still be popular in 1967? To please the masses, Festival Canada would have needed a second impresario — one with less dignified taste than Henry Wrong's, one with popular taste, an Ed Sullivan.

The statistical evidence for the success of Festival Canada is convincing. So many performances, so many organizations participating, so many premières, so many commissions. It was a comprehensive program and it succeeded in staging spectacular cultural events and entertainment and a time of celebration. It was truly a festival.

VISUAL ARTS PROGRAM

The Commission launched a Visual Arts Program designed to help art galleries and art museums develop exhibits to celebrate the Centennial. The response from galleries and museums was enthusiastic. A contemporary Centennial spin was evident in many, such as in the exhibition at the Norman MacKenzie Gallery in Alberta entitled "Canadian Art 1967," which was an exhibition of one work each by twenty artists and a catalogue containing statements or other commentary by various artists from all over Canada.

Others looked back to the past, giving Canadians a chance to understand themselves better. Typical was the University of Sherbrooke art gallery, which mounted an exhibition of Canadian paintings, sculpture, crafts and furniture from the eighteenth, nineteenth and twentieth centuries. The Commission helped them get it underway, but the show was marginal at best, partly because the criteria for receipt of a grant were not strict. Evenhandedness and generosity are expected when programs are supposed to be universal, but this approach does unfortunately leave openings for less than top-notch efforts.

The National Gallery of Canada displayed three hundred years' worth of Canadian art — the largest and most inclusive exhibition of Canadian art ever assembled. For this show, five hundred works of painting, sculpture, graphic and decorative arts were drawn from many collections, including that of the National Gallery. Unique among the works in this great exhibit were works by artists which had never been shown to the public before.

In addition to the projects undertaken by the Centennial Commission, most federal government departments and some Crown corporations such as the National Gallery of Canada carried out major programs with a Centennial theme. Some of those were undertaken especially to mark the Centennial. Others were regular programs or projects that were going to be carried out anyway.

TV AND FILM

A film program was developed by the Planning Branch, in order to give Canadians a view of themselves and to give the world an understanding of Canadians. Among other accomplishments, six films were commissioned relating to the major programs, art film libraries were established in each province by the Canadian Centre of Films on Art and a Festival of Laughter was mounted, based on an international critics' poll of the "twelve best comedy films of all time."

Air Canada sponsored no less than nine major television spectaculars, all shown on the CBC network: four in English and French, three in English only, and two in French only.

In 1966, the National Film Broad produced "Helicopter Canada," a filmed helicopter tour of the country, using a unique camera mount that controlled the negative effect of the helicopter vibrations. The film was released by Columbia of Canada and enjoyed rave reviews and a long run during 1967 in theatres throughout Canada. Canada had never before seen itself, close up, from the air.

Like "Helicopter Canada," all the other arts programs performed the classic function of theatre — that is, to hold a mirror up to an audience and let it see itself. As Canadians, we saw our emotions, our history, our collective identity on the screen, in the theatre and in the books and music that were produced with the help of the Centennial Commission. Our identity reflected upon and consolidated, we came out of 1967 stronger and better prepared to face our future.

CHAPTER *10*

Fun and Shared Experience

I F ANNIVERSARIES AREN'T FUN, THEY'RE hardly worth celebrating. All of us, at one time or another, have suffered through a dreary anniversary or birthday party — made all the more glum because it was supposed to be fun. Though Canada made room for dignity and serious reflection in its anniversary celebrations, sometimes all we needed was a good laugh. We got one on the west coast when contenders in the Great Centennial Bathtub Race bumped thirty-four miles across choppy water from Nanaimo to Vancouver on June 30. Then there were the Ottawa Stetson Strutters, who from June 24 to July 1 took the Trans-Canada Centennial Square Dance Train from Halifax to Vancouver, four hundred dancers in all. The YMCA Men's Club of Montreal staged an event that would not be fun for some, but was for the participants — a cross-country marathon. The Centennial gave us all the excuse to hold parties and generally make merry. We wanted to celebrate and we did!

And what about this for imagination? The government of the Northwest Territories decided to rig up a Centennial barge to travel the Mackenzie River some 2,500 miles, right to its mouth at Inuvik. The unique feature of the barge was a Ferris wheel to delight the children at every settlement along the way, most of whom had likely never seen one before.

At the personal level, families across the country had their own celebrations and contests. Things like the man who promised his teenaged kids he'd buy an antique car for a hundred dollars and teach them to drive it, or the man who challenged his youngest son (age twelve) to a tournament of a hundred chess games during the year. The man was me, the car was a '39 Dodge that had been painted with a broom, and the twelve-year-old won the chess tournament, 86-14. I've never played since.

Many men throughout Canada got the urge to look like their Victorian ancestors and grew beards. In some communities there were beard-growing contests.

Some of the parties on July 1, 1967, were little ones, like the foursome on the lawn beside the Library of Parliament who spread a white tablecloth on the grass and downed with gentility two bottles of Moët and Chandon White Star from cut-glass flutes. (This one was held by Art McDonald, a publicist for the National Capital Region Centennial programs.)

Other parties were bigger. The largest of all was thrown by Judy LaMarsh. It was her crowning achievement — a birthday party for kids, held on Parliament Hill on July 1, 1967. This is her description of the affair:

> ...a huge beautiful white cake (wood, not cake because it was so big, but covered with gorgeous squishy real icing), decorated with flowers and coats of arms of the provinces in colours, surmounted by the flag. Clowns dressed as animals and storybook figures roved the grounds; sparklers for the kids and a balloon for each; small stages scattered about the grounds with magic shows and a Punch-and-Judy show; and dancers accompanied by a champion fiddler; bands and flags; and slathers of food, enough that no child would be turned away.

The cake was thirty feet high. Thirty thousand portions of cake and ice cream were served to a lot of very happy kids!

ALPHA AND OMEGA

One birthday celebration led to another, and during the year five hundred people born in 1867 or before were honoured with the presentation of special certificates of recognition, distributed by their local member of Parliament. At the other end of the chart, about fifteen hundred babies born on July 1, 1967, were honoured with a special certificate. The span was dizzying: five hundred people looking back one hundred years and three times as many looking forward.

YOUTH TRAVEL

The roll call of programs, projects and events ends with one that met much of the psychic need at anniversary time, a non-competitive activity and one in which many individuals can participate — travel. One segment of society that loves to get away from home and that undoubtedly stands to benefit from seeing new places and doing new things is the younger echelon and that is the group to whom we catered.

While it was relatively inexpensive to hand out medallions and sponsor athletic competitions, it would cost a lot more to pick up the tab for gaggles of teenagers travelling from one end of the country to the other. But it could be done for some. A youth travel program under the Centennial banner and under the aegis of the Commission was a natural. After all, it was a family affair. It would be great to travel from Quebec and live with a family for a week in Alberta — and vice versa. Or from British Columbia to Nova Scotia or from New Brunswick to Saskatchewan. Gerald Poulin, section head of the Youth Travel Program, reporting to George Lee, chief of the Cultural Division, ran this program. The Commission described the goals of the program thus:

> ...to provide the opportunity to experience the variety and beauty of Canada...to obtain first-hand knowledge of the educational, industrial, political and cultural development of a part of Canada outside their home province.

It did this and also gave young Canadians practice in developing social and communication skills and in appreciating group dynamics.

Obviously the Commission could not do all the footwork needed to contact young people all over Canada, so we delegated this task to voluntary agencies like the Canadian Conference of Christians and Jews and other national, provincial, regional and local voluntary agencies. The Commission promised to provide financial assistance for these agencies to sponsor travel and exchange projects which, in the Commission's judgement, would "make a positive contribution to the celebration of the Centennial of Confederation." Projects were to be "interprovincial, home-to-home exchanges, or meetings where a significant number of the participants were from provinces other than the one where the meeting was taking place, or interprovincial tours with a cultural or historical theme, which would permit participants to meet young people en route." Fifteen thousand dollars was made available to any qualifying group in any one year to assist in paying part of the cost of travel, accommodation and meals. These loose specifications offered a great opportunity for anyone skilled in grantsmanship, and there was much potential for boondoggle. However, grants were made to assist scores of projects of the nature defined.

But the Commission needed a tighter program, more closely related to the Centennial. And so Valerie Forbes and Peter Mandia, two project officers, designed a more formal one to run parallel with the others. The selection of students to participate was administered by the provincial departments of education working through district superintendents and the principals of secondary schools. Students had to be at least fifteen years of age, and preference was given to those in their second-last year of high school who had demonstrated leadership ability, personality and academic achievement.

Each travel unit consisted of twelve boys and twelve girls, with one man and one woman as escorts. The travellers spent one week, exclusive of travelling time, during the months of

July and August 1964-67 in a province or territory other than their own. They travelled by train. Host families were selected and the travellers were guests in their homes during the visit. The local communities responsible for selecting the host families also organized a program of activities during the week-long stay.

If a group passed through Ottawa, for instance, they were given a tour of the capital region by the National Capital Commission. Groups passing through Montreal in 1967 were given a day at Expo '67. The travellers and escorts paid nothing. The experience was subsidized in full by the Centennial Commission. Each student and escort received, along with a Centennial travel bag, a Centennial identification badge, luggage stickers and luggage tag, a student escort handbook and a songbook entitled *Young Canada Sings*.

The songbook had words and music to sixty-seven perennials, leading off with "O Canada." Included were "Jack Was Every Inch a Sailor," "Greensleeves," "Waltzing Matilda" and "Joshua Fought the Battle of Jerico." It was campfire kind of stuff — not particularly Centennial. But singalongs should be unifying and the songs were what they knew. No attempt was made to drag obscure Canadian folk songs in by the heels.

There was at least one guitar player in every unit and at least one guitar. So it would not have been surprising to hear the tender strains of "This Land is Your Land" rise in the railway coach as it shook, rattled and rolled through the prairie night, headed for Newfoundland. A bit of nation-building, infinitesimal but memorable in the minds of young Canadians.

Forbes and Mandia were both young, smart, bilingual, organized, good-natured and capable. Once the principal task of liaison with the provincial authorities had been established, it all became detail. Verifying the schedule of each group and working on the logistics of the Ottawa and Montreal portions — cities to which all the students travelled.

The program was never qualitatively analyzed, but the general feeling on the part of all involved was that it was a great success.

By the autumn of 1967, the number of participants during the year and the three preceding years had reached significant proportions: 528 groups, 1,056 escorts, and 12,728 Centennial travellers. Not so infinitesimal after all.

CHAPTER 11

Public Relations

D URING JOHN FISHER'S EARLY days on the job, his advisor in the Privy Council Office had helped him develop a rudimentary organization chart. It showed he would need a director of planning, a secretary of the Commission, and a director of public relations.

Jean-Pierre Houle was the original incumbent in the position of director of public relations and the circumstances relating to his withdrawal from the position have already been recounted.

With two big special projects successfully underway, the Centennial Grants Program and the Confederation Memorial Program, and the Centennial symbol selection process started, I had worked myself out of a job. In January 1964, the board of directors rectified the situation by appointing me to succeed Jean-Pierre Houle as director of public relations.

Carrying out the responsibilities of this position became the last, the largest and the most important of my "special projects." The recruiting process had been grinding on and had produced some excellent candidates. This meant that I was able to delegate administration of the two Centennial grants programs to John Weldon, who was appointed director of the Federal Provincial Grants Branch and, as a bonus, was able to create for myself a Special Projects Branch, under Group Captain Ross Ingalls, recently retired from the Royal Canadian Air Force. After all, special projects had been a useful concept, why dispense with it?

Genius was not required to recognize that public relations would be a cardinal function. The whole concept was related to the public. The board also realized that the mammoth scale of the function could not be successfully undertaken by staff alone. Professional outside help would be required, in the form of an advertising agency. It was assumed that an advertising agency would somehow magically generate awareness and foster commitment to Centennial participation — as if the Centennial was a product they could just go out and advertise. But the problem with this thought process in 1963 was that there was no product. We didn't know what kind of program we would have. Furthermore, to introduce a new product, you have to generate the idea that there is a need for the product, to attract attention to that need and to build enthusiasm for trying out the product. These functions are the bailiwick of public relations, and with rare exceptions, advertising agencies do not have strong public relations departments.

The agency chosen by the government in 1963 was Collyer Advertising Ltd. of Montreal. It is not difficult to discover how this came about.

Advertising agencies for big government contracts are selected by the minister. There is no tender call against clear plans and specifications as there would be in the case of a building contract. Advertising agencies are selected the way people choose chiropractors. You find one who'll probably do as good a job as the next one, since they're all trained the same way. You don't advertise for a chiropractor, and you don't advertise for an advertising agency.

But something more important comes into play here. At election time when politicians need help to advertise themselves in the popularity contest, where do they turn for help in getting exposure? Generally to the one place that has the skill — an ad agency. When political parties need the same help on a regional, provincial or national basis, where do they turn? To the same place.

How do they pay for all this, since they depend on contributions from volunteers and are notoriously short of funds? Often they don't. The expense is deferred until they are elected. Then they discharge the obligation by giving government advertising contracts to those who helped them in the election war. And governments are big advertisers.

As simple as a, b, c. Collyer had helped the Liberals get back into power in the election held on April 23, 1963. Maurice Lamontagne, who was appointed secretary of state after the election, was one of those Liberals who'd run in a Montreal riding. One phone call.

"Maurice, we'd like to take a crack at this Centennial thing."

"Jim, you've got it. I'll tell Fisher. Come down to Ottawa and introduce yourself and get started."

There is nothing ethically wrong with this. One chiropractor is as good as another. No money is paid up front. Ad agencies live by creating ideas, artwork and copy, and buying media space. They then charge the client for the bought space. So much per exposure. They live by volume. The more space, the higher the fee. What's your budget for advertising? Fine. Here's how we'll spend it. Every cent.

It is hard to imagine a more dapper or charming man than Jim Collyer. Mature, idol-handsome, he oozed self-confidence. A salesman. He was welcomed with open arms at the Centennial office. We needed help and he was there to give it. But there was a problem. Jim Collyer had no idea how to help us. We didn't know what we wanted and he did not have the skill to help us find out. He was a media placer. We had nothing to place.

In visits to his office in Montreal, we would look in vain for the large creative staff we presumed were ready and able to help us crystallize our thinking, to be our partners in overcoming inertia and getting some momentum into the Centennial preparations. But they weren't there. What small staff we did find were bankrupt of ideas.

As the weeks flowed into months and the months flowed into 1963-64, we all realized that we had to get rid of Collyer and start over. As I had inherited the agency along with my new job I had to figure a way out of this mess. It is a sensitive business "relieving" an agency of an account. If they don't voluntarily withdraw, it is very damaging to their reputation if they are fired. In the end, neither of these courses was needed. Collyer Advertising Ltd. declared bankruptcy and within a month closed its office and disappeared forever.

The government was embarrassed. The minister looked sheepish. We felt abandoned. But it cleared the way for a new and different approach that would eventually lead to the largest co-ordinated network of PR and ad agencies ever assembled in Canada, to innovative methods of co-operation for ad agencies and a single-fee structure with advertising space billed at cost.

Once again, the Centennial organizers backed into the right approach. Things would have run more smoothly right from the start, however, if we had taken some time to understand the extraordinary array of functions that are part of public relations and to plan how to make those functions work for us.

Whole libraries of books have been written about public relations. The concept is based on the fact that relationships are what life is all about. An individual has to relate to other humans, to the physical universe, to himself, and in a spiritual sense, to God. Right relations in a Biblical sense are implied in the word righteousness. Bad relationships are just that — bad. My working definition of PR as it applies to corporations, governments and institutions has always been this: "The work of public relations is to get a corporation to live right and to get credit for it." The first part of this definition is the work of the executives and managers. The second part is the work of the communications department. Inherent in communication are the concepts of promotion, publicity, information, advertising, market research and marketing. PR per se is not generally perceived by the public to embrace these concepts, but in its broad definition it does include them. Each of these aspects of PR has its own array of tools and methodologies. In a real sense, PR is senior in the hierarchy of functions, senior to advertising which is generally perceived as the principal tool in the corporate inventory.

When provision was made in the establishment of the Centennial Commission for a director of public relations, the framers had little knowledge of what was really involved. They thought PR sounded like what they wanted, but director of communications might have been a better handle. Anyway, a rose by any other name. It was up to me to catch the drift and make it sweet. I had not had experience in all the functions suggested by the title I bore. But I learned.

One thing was clear: I had to start with promotion and publicity. If you want to attract attention to something, you stage a promotion. An example suggested to me by a seasoned practitioner early in my tenure was that Secretary of State Judy LaMarsh should go up a hundred feet into the air in an aerial fire ladder and paint the Centennial symbol on the wall of Toronto's Union Station. That would be a promotion. It would attract attention and get publicity for the symbol. (A good example, but in the end we did not submit Judy to the suggested indignity.)

In a sense the whole Centennial exercise was one big promotion set up to attract attention to the milestone Canada was passing. One hundred years as a modern political state.

Information is one of the substantive tools needed to relate to the public. It is the assemblage of facts that the public needs to know in order to make a choice (an informed choice) concerning participation. The participation can be passive ("Oh isn't that interesting") or active ("Hey, let's participate, let's get involved"). Information that is not disseminated is still information. A library is full of information; the Dead Sea Scrolls were full of information. But their impact was not realized until they were discovered and translated and their words disseminated.

In the context of public relations broadly defined, a process of communication is always required to get the inherent knowledge out of the jar, out of the cave. Information can never lead to attitudinal change unless it is broadcast. That is why every government department has its little army of information officers. In the context of advertising, information is not only disseminated; it is also used to persuade. In the area of government programs, paid advertising is the only certain means of ensuring that information gets to market and that it comes to the public's attention.

Of course, the public can become inured to advertising. But the creation of great advertisements is the challenge facing every ad agency. And by selective media placement, target markets can be addressed with precision.

No new commercial product or service is ever deployed before market research is done with respect to the intended user. This process ensures that the product or service will receive optimum acceptance, purchase and use. Today the techniques of public opinion polling pioneered by such men as Gallup have been refined to the point that an accurate, reliable pulse can be taken of any segment or all segments of society. Provided the questions asked are crafted with the utmost skill, the answers can contribute significantly to prudence in forming policy, including public policy.

With regard to the 1967 celebrations, no attempt was made to understand the social and psychological significance of the anniversary compulsion or to build on these underpinnings. No attempt was made to take the Canadian pulse through application of public opinion/market research techniques. It was assumed the product had been prudently chosen and would be well received. With this assumption, the concept as well as the participation in the programs and projects had to be marketed, and the tools used were in the domain of promotion, publicity, information and advertising.

The first task at hand was that of attracting the right people to do the job. To do this I followed the advice of the two generals I had worked for in my career. Both were chairmen of the National Capital Commission: Major-General Howard Kennedy and Lieutenant-General Samuel Findley Clark. Lieutenant-General Clark had said, "Peter, I don't know any way to get a job done but to find the best people you can, give them policy

The Centennial project of the famed Royal Canadian Mounted Police was a combined tour of the force's colourful musical ride and its 50-member band.

Voyageur canoe pageant on its way to Expo '67. The flotilla left Rocky Mountain House in Alberta on May 24 and paddled 3,283 miles in 104 days to reach Montreal on September 4, 1967. (FRANK GRANT/NATIONAL ARCHIVES OF CANADA/PA–185522)

Map showing route of Centennial voyageur canoe pageant (GEOFFREY FRAZER/NATIONAL ARCHIVES OF CANADA/PA–185467)

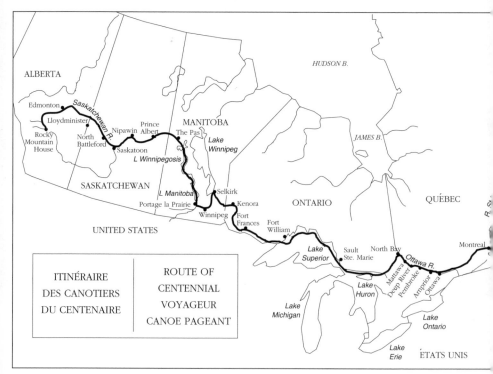

The grand finale of the Canadian Armed Forces tattoo: A lone bugler is spotlighted as he sounds the "Last Post." (MALAK/NATIONAL ARCHIVES OF CANADA/PA–185515)

Poster for the Canada-67 Tattoo (NATIONAL ARCHIVES OF CANADA/PA–183653)

One of the contestants at the Miss Canadian Indian Princess Pageant, Delia Opekokew of Saskatchewan. Photo taken in the Indian Pavilion at Expo '67
(ARMOUR LANDRY/NATIONAL ARCHIVES OF CANADA/PA–185513)

Committee for the National Indian Conference, Ottawa. Front row, left to right: Guy Williams, president, Native Brotherhood of British Columbia; Chairman Ralph Steinhauer, Brousseau, Alta.; Chief Omar Peters, Moravian Band, Ont. Back row: Chief Andrew Delisle, Caughnawaga, P.Q.; Mrs. Marian Meadmore, National Indian Council, Winnipeg; Reverend Adam Cuthand, Selkirk, Man.
(DOMINION-WIDE/NATIONAL ARCHIVES OF CANADA/PA–185479)

Indian chief, 1967 (National Archives of Canada/PA–183652)

Thirty-three Kalem gymnasts from Toronto bounced large red balls to music at the Folk Arts Festival, June 30, 1967. (Malak/National Archives of Canada/PA–185506)

Maitland Steinkopf, chairman of the Manitoba Centennial Corporation, wearing ethnic costume. Ross Lawrence, Centennial Commission regional officer, admires Mr. Steinkopf's Indian headdress, Hungarian shirt and vest, German lederhosen, Ukrainian sash, Dutch klompen and shillelagh. Winnipeg, Man., 1967
(National Archives of Canada/PA–185504)

Great International Bathtub Race, from Nanaimo to West Vancouver, July 30, 1967: Physician Howie McDiarmid set out on the SS Sacred *in a hospital gown, but quickly floundered and didn't finish the race.* (Jim Ryan/National Archives of Canada/PA–185510)

Great International Bathtub Race: Competitor Terry Pope of Victoria (Jim Ryan/National Archives of Canada/PA–185508)

Her Majesty Queen Elizabeth cuts the huge Confederation birthday cake, July 1, 1967, at the Centennial party on Parliament Hill (Dominion-Wide/National Archives of Canada/C–24559)

Expo '67 advertisements

General Charles de Gaulle during his abbreviated visit to Canada in 1967

Bobby Gimby, composer of the song "CA–NA–DA," pied-pipers a flock of schoolchildren in 1967. (MALAK/NATIONAL ARCHIVES OF CANADA/C–26756)

Tin-pan band riding in the parade at the starting ceremonies for the canoe pageant, Rocky Mountain House, Alberta (FRANK GRANT/NATIONAL ARCHIVES OF CANADA/PA–185514)

Clyde Batten, national publicity co-ordinator, Centennial Commission
(John Evans/National Archives of Canada/PA–185475)

The author in full flight, Halifax, Nova Scotia, November 21, 1965
(Maurice Crosby/National Archives of Canada/PA–185516)

Ernest A. Côté, member of the Executive Committee of the board of directors of the Centennial Commission (National Film Board/National Archives of Canada/PA–185474)

Gilles Bergeron, who succeeded Georges Gauthier as associate commissioner of the Centennial Commission in April 1967 (Studio Von Dulong/National Archives of Canada/PA–185503)

View of Expo '67, Montreal, Quebec, 1967 (NATIONAL ARCHIVES OF CANADA/C–30085)

Newspaper story featuring Quebec provincial license plates advertising the Centennial of Canadian Confederation 1867–1967
(NATIONAL ARCHIVES OF CANADA/PA–183653)

guidance, responsibility and authority, get them the money, men, material and machines they need, set up a good reporting system, and leave it up to them."

More by good luck than good management I was able to recruit people to head up each of the four functional groupings noted above, and to assemble staff. Following Lieutenant-General Clark's dictum, I gave them policy guidance, responsibility and authority, got them money, set up a good reporting system and left it up to them.

Because we had to penetrate every corner of the Canadian market, it appeared certain that we would have to hire an advertising agency. Ad agencies have the contacts and experience to buy space in every media outlet, and they employ creative talent useful in the preparation of printed and promotional material. However, few agencies at that time had a strong PR component.

The favoured agencies were asked to come and to show and tell how they would handle the account, and Vickers and Benson of Toronto were the clear choice of the Executive Committee. They did an admirable job, and during Centennial year itself helped me out of a tight spot featuring Judy LaMarsh. Early in 1967 The Honorable Ms. LaMarsh decided that some of the Commonwealth countries would like to share in Canada's Centennial experience. She could not visit them all but chose Australia as a suitable country where she could travel to recount all that was going on. Before she went away, she had complained in writing that there was not enough Centennial "awareness" advertising across the country.

As soon as she left, I schemed with Vickers and Benson to rent all the outdoor billboards between her office on Parliament Hill and her residence and plastered them with the ads we were using at the time. Upon her return, she had nothing but praise for the magnificent coverage our advertising was receiving throughout Canada.

Back in 1964, however, we were still in a corner. Vickers and Benson looked promising, but we needed an ad agency in Quebec to complement the English agency's work. When advertising in Quebec, it is essential to have the copy created and prepared in French. To create it in English and put it through a translation sieve is wrong. Errors both gross and subtle occur. Different culture. Different mindsets. To avoid this, you hire a Quebec-based, Quebec-oriented agency. We prepared a list of the agencies in Canada that had a national reach and that were known to be partisan Liberals. It would have been a waste of time to select a "Conservative" agency. Approval to appoint would never have been forthcoming.

The only agency we could find with assured Liberal credentials was Agence Canadienne in Montreal. They put on a show of enthusiasm but it became evident that what interested them most was the billings. Unlike Vickers and Benson, who were on a flat fee plus media space billed at cost, Agence Canadienne worked on billings plus a percentage.

Agence Canadienne liked the symbol because in its simple form it needed no translation, and where the graphics manual specified text and how it could be used, it was all bilingual text. Their big creative idea was to invent a snappy slogan. What they came up with to accompany all advertisements was *un nouveau départ*. Literally, a fresh start, and clearly a *double entendre*. There was no sense or expectation in the rest of Canada that, post-1967, a fresh start was needed or would occur. Did a fresh start mean to Québécois that things would be different as Confederation entered its second century? How different? In what way? I sensed an *indépendantiste* undertone. They felt smug about it, and were elated at the idea. I was trying to be accommodating and treat them gently, since our whole Commission was so heavily Anglo, so I didn't attempt to modify the slogan. The sentiment therefore appeared on all copy in French. It played well. We did not hear any objections from the Anglo and ethnic constituencies in Quebec. French-speaking federalists winked at it. French-speaking nationalists loved it. But it was not a unifying influence.

This development relates to a painful reality I had to face. I could not find a bilingual candidate with ability and stature to be my assistant, to lead the PR assault on the general indifference in Quebec toward the Centennial of Confederation. The Public Service Commission could not find anyone among the government departments — too risky. They were comfortable where they were. Paid ads in the French papers in Quebec yielded several candidates but they were not really qualified to do the job. (I did hire one for a subordinate position, however.) My mentor in Montreal, John de B. Payne, kept promising to find me someone, but months went by with no action. He was drawing a blank and I suspect he realized that no one with any fire in their belly wanted any part of it. In desperation I had to settle for a tidy, precise, nervous man named Marcel Dubuc who worked in Montreal for the CBC International Service. He could write excellent French and English and was an enthusiastic Canadian. I felt he would be loyal to me, this characteristic being one I had to have, since the potential of subverting my wishes and my federalist thrust by someone with divided loyalties was a bitter reality. He provided workmanlike, if uninspired, service, and to some degree was able to interface officially with my French-speaking constituency in Quebec, in the government and elsewhere. But he was no strategist. And he was without imagination. He had one ability of doubtful utility. He could write perfectly with either hand, and what's more, do so simultaneously. He often provided light entertainment on social occasions by accepting dictation and producing two perfect copies at once! A bonus. But not the dashing *agent provocateur* I had dreamed of having.

Thus *un noveau départ* slipped into the Centennial lexicon in Quebec unchallenged, and an opportunity to effect real lasting attitudinal change in favour of federalism was significantly compromised.

With pure advertising pinned down, the classic public relations aspect had to be taken care of. Again we called in the most respected PR agencies. One of them argued that we didn't really know what we were doing and asked for a commission to thoroughly analyze our problems. Then they would tender the job. That was a proven approach, and there was much truth in their observation, but we did not feel we had time for a two-step approach. We did not follow their advice and will never know what the result might have been.

The same was done with "French" agencies. Bouchard and Ellis of Montreal was selected: the charm and winsomeness of its presentation moved us. In making the pitch, the agency's president began: "I don't speak much England but I do the best I are." How could one not love such ingenuousness? But alas, a kind of "two solitudes" existed between us, they were not too enthused about the Centennial concept and I failed to inspire them. We used them only minimally and in 1966 and 1967 not at all.

The largest, most respected PR agency in the business, Public and Industrial Relations, (PIR), with its head office in Toronto, got the main job. They worked with us until the end, billing staff at an hourly rate and collateral materials (pamphlets, posters, explanatory booklets) at cost plus a percentage. One would have thought that Canada's largest PR agency would have the connections and credibility to cover Canada but this was not so. They cut no ice with the Halifax *Chronicle Herald* nor with the *Edmonton Journal.* What was needed was an agency with guaranteed trans-Canada connections. None existed. So we had to create one. Clyde Batten, a freelance PR man, who had been an active worker for various federal Liberal candidates during recent election campaigns, became my chief of publicity. He had been editor of the *Varsity,* the campus paper at my old alma mater, the University of Toronto. I had been an assistant editor in my day and tended to look upon editors in a manner akin to awe. He was also a Mensa. Super intelligence. A characteristic in staff that I prize above all else. He never failed me. Not once.

He was dispatched across Canada to find out how PR was done outside the Ontario and Quebec heartland. He found the most respected PR agencies in the Atlantic provinces, British Columbia and the Prairie provinces, and we commissioned one in each of these regions. Their job was to make sure our press releases would receive favourable notice and to create promotional opportunities for the events, programs and projects as they began to take shape.

Never before had this type of network been built in Canada. Clyde also persuaded the head office of Canadian Press to assign a seasoned reporter *full-time* during 1966 and 1967 to cover the unfolding story. This was a *coup*, since all the CP wire material under the byline Gerald McNeill was picked up everywhere — even outside Canada. An absolutely brilliant stroke that elevated McNeill to hero status in our eyes.

Then there were the mountains of print material that had to be cranked out to support Centennial projects and Confederation events such as the train, the caravans, the military tattoo, and the canoe pageant. The task of producing these documents was divided between PRI and Vickers and Benson, the French text being created by Agence Canadienne in Montreal. The finished artwork was taken to the Queen's Printer, who would call tenders and arrange printing and Canada-wide distribution for the millions of copies required. Leon Beauchamp, who could sniff a whiff of printer's ink six blocks away, was my superb chief of the Publications Division. For Festival Canada a separate agreement was struck with McLaren Advertising, who designed, promoted and distributed the posters and playbills for each of the elements making up Henry Wrong's mammoth impresario operation.

This part of the exercise resulted in two of the three procedural errors laid at my door during the Centennial Commission years.

The first was that the playbills contained local advertising and delays were experienced in getting them ready in some of the more remote locations such as Rimouski or Grande Prairie. Sometimes they would arrive at intermission during the first performance of a play or dance, sometimes as the curtain fell on the last performance! This made for a nasty situation. The fury of Wrong and his colleagues descended on me like a firestorm. I had no excuse. I had to take it.

The second arose because Henry Wrong, who did not work for me but for the Festival Canada Agency, would order supporting print from McLaren — banners, billboards and point-of-purchase standees. McLaren would then send the bill to me.

I had not been made part of their planning and I had failed to establish a system whereby I could give him approval for such expenditures (like the ones I had in place for all other aspects of my operation). McLaren went way beyond budget. OK, so what? Well, the "so what" was that Judy LaMarsh had a similar experience with them when she was minister of national health and welfare and here she was again humiliated by the same agency that had let her down before. She wanted my head.

I was summoned before a special meeting of the Executive Committee in what was a veritable court martial. Fisher by this time was treating me with unfriendly coldness because he realized we had reduced him to an impotent figurehead. Georges Gauthier was distinctly unsympathetic because it is a "no-no" for public servants to go beyond their budgets. As the court martial unfolded I was truly frightened. But all the other members of the Committee supported me. Ernest Côté in particular conducted a brilliant cross-examination of me, and bit by bit evidence was adduced of sufficient aggregate weight to convince the group that they could not in conscience fire me as the minister had ordered.

It took two whole days.

I had learned my lesson. Henceforth, McLaren would send me copies of Henry Wrong's requests for discussion and authorization, and, behold, Henry ceased to order material profligately and resigned himself to living within an approved budget. But I certainly had paid for his angst about the sometimes erratic and elusive playbills.

The third error related to the canoe pageant.

It will be recalled that the eight canoes followed the exact route of the fur traders. Crossing northern Ontario, they encountered a veritable hell of black-flies, portages, wild rapids and harsh rocks, and had burst out of the wilderness having been incommunicado for four days. They were at a low point. Morale was off the bottom of the chart. They searched in vain for any mention of this portion of their great feat in the *Toronto Star* and *Winnipeg Free Press*. There was none. They turned their anger on me. Wasn't I responsible for publicity for this arduous promotion? I was. My information officer attached to the pageant had done a superb job whipping up enthusiasm along the way, but without paddling with them, how could he feel their torture?

They were threatening to mutiny. They felt unappreciated and were feeling sorry for themselves. Robbins Elliot and I hastened to Wawa, a bleak way station in the middle of nowhere, and between us we succeeded in lowering the heat. But when my back was turned I could sense they wanted to beat me to a pulp with their trusty paddles.

The red carpet at Wawa was not thick enough. I hadn't realized that they truly merited a heroes' welcome.

To round out the information function, a monthly *Centennial Bulletin* was published and circulated to all known Centennial workers in Canada. As for all other pieces of print, this one was in both official languages. The format was usually the tumble form, where the first half right to the spine is in one language and when you get there and turn it upside down, you find the other language. Sometimes the print pieces were done in parallel form — that is, English text side by side with French — and once in a while, separate editions were produced, each indicating that a version in the other language was available upon request.

As an Anglophone, I had been sensitized at the National Capital Commission to the need to "not cheat those whose first language was French." This had become government policy. And about time. I enthusiastically adhered to it despite the delays and frustrations it caused. French text comes out about 10 percent longer for one thing. For another, the nuance in the French language is finer, more subtle (and more elegant) than in English, and it was common to have two competent translators differ strongly over how to say what appeared to be in English a very simple phrase. To be safe, most texts went for approval to the Translation Bureau of the secretary of state, the ultimate Canadian government authority. And they refused to be hurried. Necessary bureaucracy. Necessary delay. But excellence in communication guaranteed.

The offshore "public" was not neglected in the PR effort. One day a man turned up in my office, sent from the minister's office. He needed a job. Could I use him? It was never an order when this happened, but diplomacy and politics normally dictated a positive answer. His name was Reeves Haggen, and he had been an associate producer on the extremely popular CBC current affairs show "This Hour Has Seven Days." The producers had publicly pushed the government too hard on certain issues and in a controversial move, the CBC had terminated the show.

Reeves Haggen was from Northern Ireland, had been an officer in British Intelligence, and was one of the sanest, wittiest and most sophisticated people I had ever met.

Yes, I could use him, I said.

I asked him to go to the United Kingdom, France and the United States and find some PR agencies in those countries that could be netted into our steady stream of promotional and informational material. He accomplished this brilliantly, and it can be fairly stated that through his efforts the huge potential audience outside of Canada heard about what was happening on a regular basis.

Another vehicle used to disseminate information was the Speaker's Bureau — a pool of voluntary speech givers. Although we were rarely able to second people from government and businesses to work for us, this time Air Canada loaned us, at their expense, Ross Smythe, a seasoned communicator from their outstanding PR Department, and together with Deborah Goldfield, he spent three years lining up speakers, preparing material and matching them with requests. His work was inexpensive and effective. It took an expert, which he was.

The essential function performed by the regional PR agencies in the network built by Clyde Batten was to act as a pipeline to local media. A PR operator in Halifax, for example, spends his professional life maintaining a trust relationship with editors and newsroom staff of the local paper and the equivalent staff at the radio and TV stations. He could guarantee press interviews for anyone travelling to Halifax, always see that attention was paid to our press releases and orchestrate total coverage when the major travelling exhibits (such as Festival Canada performances and the military tattoo) hit Halifax. The key word here is trust. If he just once gave out false information, exaggerated puffery or overblown hype, all his future credibility would suffer. This is the clue to good press relations. Honesty and not making more of the material than it warrants.

One practitioner of this art was Angela Burke. She had been a crack reporter for the *Toronto Star* and we hired her as freelancer to act as liaison with the women's press in Canada. She knew the reporter's side of the trust concept and consequently was absolutely superb when dealing with women editors or women with regular bylines. We could absolutely guarantee a hearing with this constituency on any subject, and if ever a person were worth her weight in gold, it was Angela Burke.

During 1965, with two years to go before a fully operational Centennial celebration, we were often very discouraged. There did not seem to be any motion out there, any awareness that something big was being planned. All the time, however, the pervasive structure for information, publicity, promotion and advertising was being carefully built, and the process of communicating was steadily being nurtured. It was a drip-drip-drip affair. Wise counsellors all around us were saying, "Be patient. It will come." Patience. "The ability to wait or persevere without losing heart." We had to have it. *Force majeure.* There was nothing else we could do. But the absolutely agonizing thing was that we had no assurance the rock would ever crack. Would this pan-Canadian celebration fizzle? Was it a big ho-hum out there? We didn't know.

It is difficult to say when the rock of indifference shattered. But one day in 1966 it did, and all of our publics started chasing us, slavering for information, begging to get involved and crowing enthusiastically about the whole thing. It was as if they had invented it, as if it had been their discovery.

In mid-1966 from the wellsprings of creativity at Vickers and Benson came one of the most cogent, entertaining and potentially unifying ideas of all: the Centennial song.

None of us had thought of having a Centennial song. The idea was too outrageous. Governments don't sing. They don't write songs because they don't know how. On June 27, 1966, the enthusiastic, assiduous and very competent account executive at V & B, Gary Duke, called me and asked, "Peter, we think we should have a Centennial song. Our people are having jingles cooked up all the time. Do we have your authority to explore this?"

I had no objection. Exploration doesn't cost much. I said, "O.K. Be sure the line 'Canada's Birthday' doesn't creep in — remember it's the Centennial of Confederation." Some weeks later I was called to Toronto. They wanted me to hear something.

I went. As we sat in their boardroom, a slight, impish figure ran in. Not walked, ran. A green cape flowing behind, he approached the table. In his hand was a valve herald trumpet about three feet long, studded with fake rubies, emeralds and amethysts. With no introduction he played, up-tempo, sixteen bars of one of the most beautiful melodies I had ever heard. Then he played it again. All eyes were on me. No one spoke. "What's it called?" I asked. The trumpeter answered, "CA-NA-DA."

"Does it have words?" He sang the words.

I whispered to Gary Duke, "And who is this guy?" — whereupon I was introduced to Bobby Gimby, one-time member of Bert Pearl's pre-TV era Happy Gang. He was the composer of the national anthem of Malaysia and now he was the composer of the Centennial song.

Promotional ideas tumbled out.

Gimby would lead groups of children all over Canada in a kind of Pied Piper parade. The kids all singing. The song would be used as a signature at Centennial events. A TV promo would be made of Gimby and the Kids. A record would be cut. Different musical groups would be asked to do a unique version.

There was one catch. "It isn't bilingual," I said.

Gimby: "No problem, I can fix it."

Two weeks later, I returned to audit the conscientious but rather puerile attempt to bilingualize it. The whole thing was too endearing for me to get strict about equal time in all sixteen bars, and I accepted it.

I arranged for an audition for Fisher, who knew Gimby from his radio days. Fisher sold it to the Executive Committee, and then everything happened as V & B had forecast. The song swept the country, placing high on the charts and rising to gold. It became Canada's 1967 national anthem. It was sung with enthusiasm and pride. It was sung by everyone.

At the other end of the promotional spectrum were small-scale items developed by my staff: flags and pins. The flag and pin lady was Sheila Stiven, a very intelligent and hard-working Scottish-born arts and crafts type from Nova Scotia who, like Clyde and many others, just turned up at the door. It was rightly divined that people would want something to wave and something to wear that would say, "Hey, look at me. We're celebrating our Centennial." Six products evolved:

- a six-by-six-inch table flag on a little post with a round wooden stand
- a series of larger flags running up to six by three feet
- a tiny coloured plastic pin mounted on a descriptive card
- a tiny brass pin mounted on a descriptive card
- tie tacks
- enamel brooches

All bore the Centennial symbol, which occupied the whole field of the object in each case.

People love buttons. Especially if they are free. The appetite to identify with the Centennial was so strong that the preliminary orders were sucked up like a late July rain in the vegetable garden. Their popularity can be gauged by these distribution numbers:

Plastic pins	1,000,000	Enamel brooches	50,000
Brass pins	1,000,000	Table flags	100,000
Tie tacks	50,000	Large flags	10,000

The largest distributors were federal members of Parliament. While we were busy shipping the stuff out to our provincial counterparts, Judy LaMarsh hit on the idea, "Why not give MPs all they want and they can take them to their constituencies and hand them out?" As bureaucrats we hated to see our precious promo material put indiscriminately into the hands of politicians, but how myopic and conceited we were. It was perfect. The MPs took them everywhere in Canada. The minister was loved for her generosity in handing out quantities of items that were perceived to be of value, and we felt justified in having dreamt up the objects in the first place.

I had a vision of many an MP sitting privately in his office on the Hill and, like Croesus, letting thousands of little gold-like Centennial pins run through his or her fingers. Enough to make politics worthwhile after all?

Flags and pins were definitely a successful idea. Quality control was high. The manufacturers produced and delivered on time. Everyone was happy.

Little pins mean a lot.

What meant a lot to Bobby Gimby is that he was made a Companion of the Order of Canada.

What meant a lot to Agence Canadienne, Vickers and Benson and Public and Industrial Relations is that, among them, they won a combined eighteen awards from their professional associations for excellence in print, radio and TV material produced for Centennial.

And what meant a lot to me was that Lieutenant-General Clark's dictum had proven correct. My combined PR forces had helped ensure a once-in-a-hundred-year triumph.

12

Expo '67

NO ACCOUNT OF THE FESTIVITIES in Canada in 1967 would be complete without consideration of Expo '67. It can be thought of as a World's Fair, but the Bureau International des Expositions in Paris, which grants permission to hold these things, has for many years permitted them to have colloquial names. The official title was *Exposition universelle et internationale de 1967*, with the theme *Terre des Hommes/Man and His World*. The short version was explicit, bilingual and catchy — Expo '67 — derived directly from the official title.

In 1960, when the first Centennial stirrings were being felt in Canada, other stirrings of an ominous nature were going on in Quebec — nationalist, separatist stirrings. Québécois were not especially interested in the Centennial because 1967 was not the centennial of their nation. They had been here since 1642, so 1967 was no birthday for them. It might be considered the one-hundredth birthday of a new political entity, but not of a nation.

Real politik therefore dictated that the federal government had to come up with some action that would be positive in impact and that would assuage the rancour of Québécois who would be offended by too much emphasis on Centennial in Quebec. The federal government made every effort to make links between this Quebec-based world's fair and the Centennial celebrations.

The federal Act establishing the Exposition, for instance, makes it plain that it was being held "in connection with the Celebration of the Centennial of Confederation in Canada." And the official literature was redolent of the spirit of anniversary underpinnings:

> The Montreal Universal and International Exhibition's aim is to provide an explanation of the world we live in to each and every one of its visitors, so that they may realize that we are jointly and severally answerable for and to each other, and that what divides men is infinitely less important than that which links them together... . It will be proof for future generations that — in this year of Canada's Centennial [*sic*] — we strive with all our might to prepare for them a future of happiness, prosperity and freedom.

The idea of a universal exhibition as a fitting way to celebrate the Centennial was first suggested by Conservative Senator Mark Drouin on his return from Brussels, where the 1958 World's Fair had been held. The idea had a lot to commend it. It would be good for Canadian pride, which was running pretty high anyway; it could be funded, because at the time the government's budgets were usually balanced; but more important it would be good for Quebec pride if it could be held in Montreal, arguably Canada's première metropolis at the time. It might help anchor Quebec into Confederation. In other words, it would meet a key anniversary goal —to analyze destructive forces and plan aggressively to oppose them.

In 1962, a Crown corporation, Expo '67, was created by an Act of Parliament, *The Canadian World Exhibition Corporation Act*. The federal government would pay 50 percent of the cost, the province $37\frac{1}{2}$ percent and the Montreal area municipal governments $12\frac{1}{2}$ percent.

Expo '67 was a mega project on a scale equal to the construction of the transcontinental railway or the St. Lawrence Seaway. The whole enterprise was beautifully conceived,

planned, designed and brilliantly executed. The impetus generated by the fair accelerated construction of Montreal's underground Métro, which was mostly completed in 1966, with 15 $\frac{1}{2}$
miles of lines. In preparation for the upcoming exposition,
Montreal also constructed the Concordia Bridge, which was
2,265 feet long and 94 feet wide, and Place des Arts, the magnificent performing arts facility in downtown Montreal. A new
island, Ile Ste-Hélène, was constructed, and Ile Notre-Dame was
doubled in size: 15 million tons of rock and earth were trucked
in; 6.8 million tons were dredged from the river bottom.

Expo '67 was a 1967 earth-shaking event, and its repercus-
sions were felt by both the Canadian Centenary Council and
the Centennial Commission. These organizing bodies had difficulty generating Centennial interest within Canadian businesses.
Where were they? Why didn't they pick up on Centennial as an
opportunity for good PR or even as an opportunity to indulge
in some self-serving and some self-interest. Why? Because they
went to Expo.

All the major Canadian corporations and hundreds of minor
ones participated in Expo. Some, like Air Canada and Polymer
Corporation, had their own pavilions; others, like Canadian
General Electric Company and Cincinnati Milling Machine
Company, sponsored some aspect of the Exposition. Others
were represented by their trade association: the Canadian
Brewer's Association, for instance, represented Canadian brew-
ers by sponsoring the Brewer's Pavilion.

The reasons are clear. Expo was site-specific and time-specific.
It was prestigious, underwritten by three levels of government and it guaranteed maximum exposure not only to millions of Canadians but also to millions of internationals. Expo
was a place to show not only the corporate flag, but also the
national flag of patriotism. Not to back Expo would have been
unpatriotic. Here the anniversary compulsion was exhibited to
perfection. Businesses knew they had no choice but to be
there. And of course it also made good business sense to show
up at the world exhibition. The total number of private sector
participants was 468.

The brilliance of Expo was its international character. Sixty foreign national governments had pavilions, as did twenty-eight member countries of the Organization for Economic Co-operation and Development (OECD). The mix was enriched by the participation of three individual states of the United States, ten Canadian provinces, the Yukon Territory and the Indians of Canada.

Ninety-two heads of state, prime ministers, premiers and governors attended, including Her Majesty Queen Elizabeth and HRH the Duke of Edinburgh, His Imperial Majesty the Sha Hansha Aryamentes of Iran and Lyndon B. Johnson, president of the United States. And there were 50,306,648 others who paid to get in.

According to information provided by the International Exhibitions Bureau in Paris and confirmed by John Allwood in his book *The Great Exhibitions*, Expo '67 was the largest and most expensive six-month exhibition ever held up to that date. The quantitative measure was total attendance and aggregate cost. (Expo '70, the Japan World Exposition, surpassed Expo '67; it welcomed 64,218,770 visitors and turned a profit of $67,816,172,00.)

There was an atmosphere of excitement, optimism and just plain fun at Expo. Celebrations are supposed to be fun and carnival is expected in mega-anniversary celebrations. The Expo organizers knew this and provided a midway, including Ferris wheels, a go-cart track and flume rides.

The Expo organization was headed by Pierre Dupuy, an ex-ambassador to France, whose title for the occasion was Ambassador and Commissioner General. It was his task initially to persuade foreign countries to commit to participation.

He had no difficulty attracting staff. As a Crown corporation, Expo was not restricted by public service guidelines and so had the liberty to set its own salaries. That, and the attraction of being associated with such a prestigious event, was a powerful magnet. Robert Shaw, an engineer, was deputy commissioner general and vice-president of the corporation. A big man in every way, he had come from the Foundation Company of

Canada. He built the physical plant for Expo and ran it after-ward. His principal delegate was Andrew Kniewasser, general manager, an ultra-smart, hard-driving individual, who had been an assistant deputy minister in the federal Department of Industry, Trade and Commerce. It was clear to all that he was the manager. He managed everything. A herculean task. The director of public relations was Yves Jasmin, on loan from Air Canada, one of Canada's most respected PR operators.

The staff was large by necessity and the demographic mix was a reflection of that of Quebec itself. Here were found the Laurendeaus, Gobeils, Saraults, Benoits, Lacombes and Martels in profusion, with a light sprinkling of Pecks, Pickards and Scotts.

Eleven advisory committees were struck to guide the plan-ners on everything from fine arts to medicine to agriculture and youth. The theme was, after all, "Man and His World." The best advice in Canada was there for the asking. Expo '67? Glad to help. What can I do?

There were times during the 1963-66 period when the offi-cials and staff of the Centennial Commission felt like poor cousins. Expo was so big, so appealing, so clearly headed for success that it discouraged those who were plodding away on the less focused, something-for-everyone program of the Commission. But these feelings were fleeting. Relations with the Expo staff were cordial, indeed fraternal. There was a sense of "all being in it together." There was no spirit of competition, though Expo did siphon off attention and some Centennial commitment, but then the occasion had become grand enough in the minds of Canadian participants that it could stand dilu-tion, diversity and more than one simple focus.

Two final statistical observations. Expo '67 cost the federal treasury $560,856,580 in 1992 dollars, whereas the Centennial Commission disbursed $359,456,592 in 1992 dollars. The Centennial Commission program costs are set out in Appendices I, J, K and L.

One is therefore tempted to ask, "Was Expo worth $200 mil-lion more than the general Centennial observances?" But this is not really a valid question. The two complemented each other. It is not possible to quantify the objective results of each.

What is of interest, however, is the geographic origin of attendees at Expo:

Montreal	26.9%
Quebec (outside Montreal)	4.8%
Canada (outside Quebec)	19.8%
United States	44.8%
Other countries	3.7%

Canadian self-determination and national pride are always given a boost when people outside Canada talk about us, and especially if they talk favourably. Americans reacted favourably to us in 1967. Look at the number who attended the show.

For Canadians, Expo was a source of great pride. Look what we've done! The world has come to us! For Québécois, it had to be an even greater source of pride. The "we" in "look what we've done" was a Quebec "we." Here was a concrete, monumental example of the fruits of Quebec's Quiet Revolution.

A new and different generation of Québécois and Québécoise was aborning during these years, and Expo '67 was a confirmation of that. The "we are" in the identity analogy achieved new dimensions.

The Expo '67 celebration was good for Canada.

It was fabulous for Quebec.

13

Tidying Up the Battlefield

A LTHOUGH CENTENNIAL ACTIVITIES in every part of Canada proceeded apace right until the last day of 1967, the two leaders of the Centennial Commission departed before it was over.

Starting in 1965, the contributions of Commissioner John Fisher became counter-productive. He began picking at the fringes of programs, demanding impossible changes; tried to interject new ideas when it was too late; attempted to subvert junior staff who were flattered by his attention; and generally became a major disruptive influence. Querulous and petulant, he began behaving like a bear with a sore paw, and his countenance and behaviour resembled a thunderstorm about to happen.

He would demand that things be done his way. Georges Gauthier would disagree and say they had to be done another way. Either way, in agreeing with one, the staff would ergo be disagreeing with the other. But Gauthier was *persona grata* with the minister, and Fisher was not, so staffers started to gravitate toward Gauthier. Then the notion gradually developed that Fisher had to be kept out of the office. I was approached informally by emissaries from the government to find a way to do so.

For a while he had an executive assistant, Jack Golding, who had been a compatriot of his from New Brunswick. Jack travelled with him from time to time and trips were arranged to eat up ten days or two weeks. When Jack, to his relief, was made regional officer in British Columbia, John recruited Lou Lapointe, who was a good-hearted soul but over his head in such a position. Lou used to come boldly into the office and demand that John wanted this or that. No one paid any attention to him. He was like a friendly terrier whose wagging tail indicated he didn't really expect us to jump when he barked.

It finally dawned on us that the most effective method to keep John on the road would be to line him up with speaking engagements back to back for months at a time and to appoint an officer whose full-time job was to travel with him, arrange press, TV and radio interviews, and to arrange for all the creature comforts he needed to swan around in relative leisure. The main point was to keep him out of the office. Floyd Caza was the man. A seasoned PR operator with National Defence (a major), he had just returned from Army HQ in Germany and relished this new management role. Caza was a delight. He was very fond of John and a true professional. He performed superbly.

The plan worked. Once in a while when John would call from Florida, London (England), Vancouver or wherever, to see what was going on, he would learn that certain actions had been taken contrary to his orders (because Georges Gauthier had countermanded them). And when he was told that since he was not here to discuss the matter, we had proceeded along such and such a line, his standard retort was, "Have you never heard of Alexander Graham Bell?" But we didn't call him when he was on the road. We didn't want to. We didn't need to.

Confusion reigned when he hit the office. Calm descended when he left. An interesting footnote to the story of this incessant ulterior-motive-designed travel is that he seldom submitted an expense account. Since he had been executive director of the Canadian Travel Association, every carrier, hotelier and restaurateur in Canada and many in the United States welcomed him when he travelled, and out of gratitude for past associations beneficial to them, they wouldn't think of having him pay the bill. He boasted how much he had saved the government and it was true. An odd circumstance that the private sector heavily subsidized his non-function as commissioner.

Caza's name never appeared in the records; he was hired through Glenn Gilbert and Associates, my vehicle for retaining John de B. Payne. His invoices read only "For Services Rendered." Caza was one of the services. This was one invoice that I knew would never be challenged. Everyone in government knew what was going on.

As Centennial wound down, Prime Minister Pearson was considering fixing John up with an appointment after 1967. After all, he held deputy minister rank and had tried to serve the country well in what he could do best — speaking. But no offer was forthcoming and he left in October to take a job in Edmonton.

Associate Commissioner Georges Gauthier left earlier than Fisher, in April 1967, to take up the post that was promised him — deputy head of the Public Service Staff Relations Board. He was succeeded immediately by a brash, perfectly bilingual young civil engineer from Quebec City, Gilles Bergeron, who had supervised the expansion of the physical plant of Quebec's burgeoning education system. Now, he was overseeing a program that was already functioning smoothly, and eventually, he presided over the swift dissolution of the whole exercise. He accepted the job on the understanding that he would have a hand in effecting the federal government's planned expansion into post-secondary education. This expansion did not occur, and he became project manager of the government's communication satellite program before returning quietly to Quebec in August 1968. He appeared to treat his job as some kind of joke, and the activities of the Commission as risible. This attitude and his pre-emptory manner were hard to take, but his seniority in the organization had to be respected.

The three senior officers remained until the last day. Claude Gauthier, the secretary, was appointed secretary of the Canada

Council, a prestigious post which he filled with distinction until his retirement. Robbins Elliott, the director of planning, became assistant director of the Pay Research Bureau and later went on to run the Exhibition Commission, the group that had done such a spectacular job designing and building the train and caravans. After stints in the Office of Design in the Department of Industry, Trade and Commerce and the Housing Design Council, he returned to the Royal Architecture Institute of Canada, retiring in 1986.

Following 1967 John Fisher and Georges Gauthier as well as all the senior staff at Expo were all admitted as Officers of the Order of Canada in recognition of their work. Robbins was not. A serious injustice, considering his signal contribution to Centennial in Canada.

As for me, in April of 1967, when Georges Gauthier was packing up, I approached him about my future. What could I expect after 1967?

He admitted, yes, he had fixed up Claude Gauthier and Robbins Elliott. But with his sly little smile, he put me in what he thought was the right place: "Well, Peter, we all know it wasn't you who did all the work. It was the PR and ad agencies; I don't think you can expect much." Georges was already thinking like the administrative tribunal judge he was about to become.

The war was over. Nothing left to do but put away the uniform and melt down the armour. Who had the inclination or the time to look after the veterans? New wars were commanding attention. "The tumult and the shouting dies, the Captains and the Kings depart." It was ever thus.

Anyone planning to put time, energy and emotion into a mega-anniversary should take heed. And yet and yet. On the other side of the balance, on the other side of caution and foresight and self-preservation, sits adventure, excitement and the chance to contribute to incremental positive growth, to evolution, the chance of a lifetime. There was a consensus throughout Canada that the Centennial celebrations had been a success. Pleasurable memories remained for all Canadians.

Although we had not articulated them, we had generally followed the ten precepts in *The Anniversary Axiomatique* and so had produced the desired effect.

We reinforced Canada's identity and proclaimed it to the world. Continuity and restatement appeared in the form of programs and publications that reminded us of our shared past. We accentuated unifying elements and opposed destructive forces at least to some degree. We pointed Canadians to the future, encouraged personal and community improvement, built monuments and memorials, and gave gifts. And finally, 1967 was a year of public performance, dignified ritual and just plain fun — a chance for Canadians, reserved and otherwise, to celebrate with warmth and optimism.

The country grew. The people grew.

Any family, institution, organization or country, when stirred by the need to celebrate an anniversary, should look to these same precepts. The weight given to each may vary with the culture and character of the celebrating parties, but the essentials are there. If you build on this anatomy of an anniversary, the success of your celebration will be as predictable as the anniversary compulsion that started it all.

Turn back to the end of Chapter 1. Photocopy *The Anniversary Axiomatique* and pin a copy to the wall in your planning committee office. You won't find any better guidance anywhere.

Happy Anniversary!

Appendices

APPENDIX A

MEMBERS OF THE CENTENNIAL COMMISSION BOARD OF DIRECTORS

The other members of the board of directors, not members of the Executive Committee, were:

Norman MacKenzie, C.M.G., M.M. and Bar, L.L.D., Vancouver, B.C.
Had been president of the Canadian Centenary Council. He attended very few meetings of the board but when he did his wisdom and broad span of reference commanded great respect from all his co-members.

Hugh O. Mills, M.B.E., Halifax, N.S.
One of John Fisher's nominees, he owned women's ready-to-wear stores. A twinkling personality, he took great interest in all that was being done.

Fred G. McGuiness, Brandon, Manitoba
A newspaper publisher, very alert, full of common sense, he accurately read and interpreted the ethos of western Canada.

George Metcalfe, Toronto, Ontario
One of Fisher's heroes and justifiably so. He was a protégé of Garfield Weston; president of Loblaws Groceterias. A very shrewd businessman who taught a weekly men's Bible class. Gifted.

Lorenzo Paré, Ottawa, Ontario
A newspaper editor from Quebec, later active in Press Council affairs. A strong federalist, he did not argue assuagement of the Quebec nationalists but seemed to feel the logic of the status quo *would prevail.*

Douglas Hunt, Q.C., St. John's, Newfoundland
A lawyer, well tuned into the mind and spirit of "Canada's Overseas Dominion" (as some called it), he provided steady advice on all Newfoundland Centennial matters.

Two excellent 1963 Fisher nominees attended only two meetings. Resigning of their own accord were Paul Desmarais, Montreal, and Richard Murray, Winnipeg. The former already a mogul, later to head up and be majority owner of the great Power Corporation, the latter head of the Hudson's Bay Company in Canada. Both probably felt the affairs of the fledgling Centennial Commission a bit thin to occupy their patently enormous talent and energy.

The members of the board of directors were all staunch Canadians. As a whole, they were an impressive group. A model pool of talent. Quebec was under-represented in the general membership, however, although Georges Gauthier tried valiantly to compensate for this weakness.

APPENDIX B

BUDGETING PROCESS

Public servants are trained to spend money, not make it. The process by which decisions are made on the amount of money desired or required is rigorous, quite simple, and based on largely unverifiable assumptions.

The Assumptions

a) That the programs and projects being proposed will be accepted by Treasury Board;

b) That no major changes on the part of the government, the minister, the deputy minister and others will take place between the time the estimate is made and the time when authority to disburse funds occurs;

c) That the costs proposed to be incurred have been calculated reasonably accurately.

Planning Document

A branch director has to submit ball-park figures of financial requirements (and much of this is a wish list) twenty-four months before funds are released.

Treasury Board

Officers in the Treasury Board review and challenge every line item, one objective being to find where cuts can be made.

Disbursement

Eventually, estimates are approved at Treasury Board. They are then debated in a committee of the House of Commons (which is a perfunctory performance), included in the annual budget of the government, and approved by Parliament to take effect at the start of the fiscal year. Departments are then free to commit to spend and to disburse.

The Centennial Exercise

Our financial needs were guesstimates. Treasury Board did not gainsay our proposals. We received the funds we thought we needed. The assumptions noted above in our case proved correct. It was really quite simple.

On March 31, 1968, we actually turned back $315,001 in unspent funds.

APPENDIX C

CENTENNIAL GRANTS PROJECTS BY PROVINCE
1967 dollars

Province	Number of Projects Approved	Federal - Centennial Grant	Provincial Centennial Grant	Total Estimated Cost
Nfld.	104	$473,589	$473,844	$2,647,618
P.E.I.	21	56,268	56,268	395,456
N.S.	37	750,720	750,719	3,622,025
N.B.	64	550,384	550,384	3,091,597
P.Q.	70	5,303,333	6,216,000	15,910,000
Ont.	666	4,879,470	4,879,470	26,174,784
Man.	181	742,692	1,611,877	5,238,245
Sask.	475	856,917	1,288,577	13,649,157
Alta.	398	1,370,396	1,370,396	8,978,224
B.C.	275	1,493,899	896,096	8,423,776
Yukon	10	27,558	51,442	178,000
N.W.T.	--	--	--	--
Totals	**2,301**	**$16,505,226**	**$18,145,073**	**$88,308,882***

* The balance of the cost not covered by the federal and provincial Centennial grants was provided by local sources, with assistance in some projects from other federal and/or provincial programs.

APPENDIX D

CENTENNIAL GRANTS PROJECTS BY CATEGORY: CANADA
1967 dollars

Category	Number of Projects	Federal - Centennial Grant	Total Estimated Cost
Historic Buildings Restoration	32	$339,618	$1,119,384
Museums and Art Galleries	67	1,017,137	4,265,369
Theatres/Performing Arts Centres	5	496,229	2,051,660
Technical Display Buildings	3	607,632	3,370,000
Libraries	137	1,602,622	10,915,298
Parks	524	3,179,277	11,230,880
Recreational Areas	299	824,363	4,156,225
Municipal Buildings	174	574,712	3,967,428
Recreational Structures	520	2,886,020	21,375,645
Erection of Memorials	30	97,481	326,993
Historical Books	38	48,642	205,862
Welfare Buildings	35	149,005	6,454,484
Community Centres	428	4,614,294	18,654,798
Conservatory	1	44,742	135,000
Bells, Chimes, Carillons	1	5,540	17,010
Restoration of Historic Trails	1	1,167	3,500
Town Clock, Clock Tower	3	1,786	5,358
Paintings, Sculptures, etc.	2	2,959	11,000
Band Instruments	1	12,000	42,988
Totals	**2,301**	**$16,505,226**	**$88,308,882**

APPENDIX E

Anne of Green Gables:
Charlottetown Festival's musical version of Lucy Maud Montgomery's famous novel of the same name. Story by Donald Harron, music by Norman Campbell, choreography by Alan Lund.

Don Messer and the Islanders:
Popular old-time country music group from the Maritimes known to millions of Canadians through television, radio, recordings and public appearances.

Holiday Theatre:
Canada's most exciting and widely known children's theatre company, with headquarters in Vancouver.

Les Feux Follets:
Canada's youthful National Folk Dance Company, with headquarters in Montreal. Les Feux Follets, *in English, is "Fabled Fireflies."*

Le Théâtre du Nouveau Monde:
Canada's oldest permanent theatre company toured its production of Terre D'Aube *by French Canadian playwright Jean-Paul Pinsonneault during 1967.*

National Ballet of Canada:
One of the world's major ballet companies, it performed The Nutcracker *and* La Sylphide *on its countrywide tour in 1967.*

National Theatre of Great Britain (London, England):
The company, directed by Sir Laurence Olivier, performed John Mortimer's English version of Georges Faydeau's A Flea in Her Ear, *and William Congreve's* Love in Canada *during 1967.*

National Youth Orchestra

New York Philharmonic (New York, U.S.):

This world-famous orchestra performed in Canada during 1967 under the direction of conductor Leonard Bernstein.

Neptune Theatre:

This Halifax company presented The Sleeping Bag *by Nova Scotian playwright Dr. Arthur L. Murphy and Sean O'Casey's* Juno and the Paycock *on its first national tour.*

Stratford Festival Company:

Recognized as North America's foremost classical theatre company, the company performed Shakespeare's Twelfth Night *and Gogoi's* The Government Inspector *on its road tour.*

APPENDIX F

1967 CONFEDERATION TRAIN ITINERARY

British Columbia
January 9 – February 21

1. Victoria
2. Nanaimo
3. Vancouver CPR Station
4. Vancouver CNR Station
5. Chilliwack
6. Kamloops
7. Kelowna
8. Castlegar
9. Cranbrook
10. Prince Rupert
11. Prince George

Alberta
February 22 – March 25

12. Jasper
13. Edmonton CNR Station
14. Edmonton Ex. Grounds
15. Red Deer
16. Calgary Central
17. Calgary Victoria Park
18. Lethbridge
19. Medicine Hat

Saskatchewan
March 27 – April 21

20. Swift Current
21. Moose Jaw
22. Saskatoon
23. North Battleford
24. Prince Albert
25. Regina

Manitoba
April 22 – May 13

26. Brandon
27. Neepawa
28. Dauphin
29. Portage la Prairie
30. Winnipeg CNR Station
31. Winnipeg St. James
32. St. Boniface

Ontario
May 14 – August 25

33. Kenora
34. Fort William
35. Port Arthur
36. Sault Ste. Marie
37. Sudbury
38. North Bay
39. London
40. Windsor
41. Kitchener
42. Ottawa Alta Vista
43. Ottawa West Station
44. Peterborough
45. Hamilton
46. Niagara Falls
47. Toronto CNE
48. Toronto Downsview
49. Toronto Danforth
50. Toronto Leaside
51. Toronto John St.
52. Kingston

Quebec (Part One)
August 26 – September 30

53. Montreal, Dorval
54. Montreal West Station
55. Westmount Station
56. Côte Vertu
57. Montreal Park Avenue
58. Papineau Piggyback Yard
59. Montreal East
60. Trois-Rivières CPR Station
61. Chicoutimi
62. Quebec City Palais Station
63. Quebec City Wolfe's Cover

Nova Scotia
October 2 – 19

64. Truro
65. Sydney
66. Halifax
67. Yarmouth
68. Kentville
69. Amherst

Prince Edward Isand
October 20 – 24

70. Charlottetown
71. Summerside

New Brunswick
October 26 – November 9

72. Moncton
73. Saint John
74. Fredericton
75. Chatham
76. Campbellton

Quebec (Part Two)
November 10 – December 5

77. Rimouski
78. Thetford Mines
79. Sherbrooke
80. St. Jean
81. Montreal Lachine
82. Montreal Central Station
83. Montreal Windsor Station

APPENDIX G

1967 CONFEDERATION CARAVANS ITINERARY

Caravan 1

Nova Scotia

North Sydney
New Waterford
Louisbourg
Baddeck
Cheticamp
Inverness
Port Hawkesbury
West Arichat
Guysborough
Antigonish
New Glasgow
Stellarton
Sheet Harbour
Middle
Musquodoboit
Musquodoboit
  Harbour
Dartmouth
Lunenburg
Bridgewater
Liverpool
Shelburne
Meteghan River
Digby
Middleton
Wolfville
Windsor
Stewiacke
Parrsboro
Springhill
Pugwash
Tatamagouche
Pictou

Prince Edward Island

Murray River
Montague
Souris
Morell
North Rustico
Kensington
O'Leary
Wellington
Borden

New Brunswick

Sackville
Shediac
Petitcodiac
Sussex
Hampton
St. George
St. Andrews
St. Stephen
Harvey Station
Oromocto
Minto
Nashwaaksis
Woodstock
East Florenceville
Andover
Grand Falls
St. Leonard
Edmunston
St. Quentin
Dalhousie
Jacquet River
Bathurst
Caraquet
Shippegan
Tracadie
Doakton
Richibucto
Newcastle

Newfoundland

St. John's
Ferryland
St. Mary's
Placentia
Whitbourne
Harbour Grace
Frenchman's Cove
Clarenville
Bonavista
Terra Nova Park
Gander
Lewisporte
Grand Falls
Buchans
Springdale
Baie Verte
Norris Point

St. Anthony
Hawke Bay
Corner Brook
Stephenville
Robinsons
Port-aux-Basques

Québec

Caravan 2

Huntingdon
Valleyfield
Beauharnois
Laprairie
St-Lambert
Longueuil
St-Hyacinthe
Sorel
Nicolet
Victoriaville
Plessisville
Manseau
Deschaillons
Ste-Croix
Charny
Lévis
Lauzon
Montmagny
St-Pamphile
St-Jean-Port-Joli
Ste-Anne-de-la-
    Pocatière
Sully
Cabano
Rivière-du-Loup
Trois-Pistoles
Mont-Joli

Sayabec
Amqui
Causapscal
Metapédia
St-Omer
Bonaventure
Chandler
Gaspé
Gros Morne
Murdochville
Ste-Anne-des-Monts
Matane
Ste-Marie
St-Georges
Lac-Mégantic
Disraeli
Asbestos
Drummondville
Actonvale
Richmond
Windsor Mills
East Angus
Coaticook
Magog
Waterloo
Sutton
Cowansville
Granby
Farnham
Bedford
Iberville
Napierville

Caravan 3

Hull
Buckingham
Lachute

Rigaud
Vaudreuil
Pte-Claire
Ste-Dorothée
St-Eustache
Ste-Thérèse
Ste-Rose
St-Vincent-de-Paul
Terrebonne
L'Assomption
Joliette
Louiseville
Cap-de-la-Madeleine
Shawinigan Falls
Grand'Mère
La Tuque
Ste-Anne-de-la-
    Pérade
Donnacona
Beauport
Ste-Anne-de-Beaupré
Baie-St-Paul
La Malbaie
Tadoussac
Forestville
Pentecôte
Sept-Iles
Baie-Comeau
Port-Alfred
Arvida
Kénogami
Jonquière
Alma
Mistassini
St-Félicien
Roberval
Chibougamau

Senneterre
Val-d'Or
Amos
La Sarre
Noranda
Rouyn
Ville-Marie
Temiscaming
Shawville
Wakefield
Maniwaki
Mont-Laurier
St-Jovite
Ste-Agathe
St-Donat
Rawdon
St-Jérôme

Ontario

Caravan 4

Rockland
Alfred
Hawkesbury
Alexandria
Casselman
Cornwall
Morrisburg
Winchester
Kemptville
Prescott
Brockville
Gananoque
Smiths Falls
Perth
Carleton Place
Arnprior

Renfrew
Pembroke
Petawawa
Chalk River
Deep River
Eganville
Barrys Bay
Bancroft
Marmora
Tweed
Napanee
Picton
Belleville
Trenton
Campbellford
Cobourg
Port Hope
Bowmanville
Oshawa
Whitby
Lindsay
Bobcaygeon
Minden
Gravenhurst
Parry Sound
Bracebridge
Huntsville
South River
Powassan
Mattawa
Sturgeon Falls
Coniston
Capreol
Lively
Espanola
Little Current
Mindemoya

Elliot Lake
Blind River
Thessalon
Wawa
Chapleau
Manitouwadge
Marathon
Terrace Bay
Nipigon
Beardmore
Geraldton
Hearst
Kapuskasing
Cochrane
Ansonville
Timmins
Kirkland Lake
Virginiatown
Englehart
New Liskeard
Haileybury

Caravan 5

Richmond Hill
Newmarket
Alliston
Barrie
Orillia
Midland
Collingwood
Shelburne
Orangeville
Arthur
Mount Forest
Listowel
Walkerton
Hanover

Markdale
Meaford
Owen Sound
Wiarton
Southampton
Kincardine
Wingham
Goderich
Seaforth
Stratford
Woodstock
Simcoe
Brantford
Galt
Preston
Waterloo
Fergus
Guelph
Georgetown
Brampton
Port Credit
Oakville
Milton
Burlington
Dundas
Ancaster
Grimsby
St. Catharines
Thorold
Welland
Fort Erie
Port Colborne
Dunnville
Caledonia
Tillsonburg
Ingersoll
St. Mary's

Exeter
Strathroy
Sarnia
Wallaceburg
Dresden
Thamesville
Glencoe
St. Thomas
West Lorne
Chatham
Tillbury
Leamington
Amherstburg
Essex

Ontario, Manitoba, Saskatchewan

Ontario

Caravan 6

Atikokan
Sioux Lookout
Dryden
Red Lake
Fort Frances
Rainy River

Manitoba

Emerson
Altona
Morris
St. Pierre
Steinbach
Ste. Anne
Beausejour
Lac-du-Bonnet

Pine Falls
Selkirk
Stonewall
Teulon
Gimli
Arborg
Ashern
Lundar
Elie
Carman
Winkler
Morden
Manitou
Clearwater
Killarney
Boissevain
Deloraine
Melita
Reston
Virden
Souris
Wawanesa
Glenboro
Treherne
St. Claude
Austin Ag. Museum
Gladstone
McCreary
Ste-Rose-du-Lac
Wasagaming
Minnedosa
Carberry
Rivers
Hamiota
Shoal Lake
Birtle
Russell

Roblin
Grandview
Ethelberg
Winnipegosis
Swan River
Snow Lake
Thompson
Flin Flon
The Pas
Hudson Bay
Carrot River
Nipawin
Tisdale
Melfort
Wakaw
Rosthern
Waskesiu
Shellbrook
Big River
Spiritwood
Meadow Lake
St. Walburg
Lloydminster
Macklin
Unity
Wilkie
Kerrobert
Kindersley
Eston
Rosetown
Outlook
Riverhurst
Davidson
Allan
Lanigan
Humboldt
Wynyard

Foam Lake
Kelvington
Preeceville
Hamsack
Canora
Yorkton
Ituna
Melville
Langenburg
Esterhazy
Moosomin
Grenfell
Indian Head
Fort Qu'Appelle
Strasbourg
Lumsden
Kipling
Carlyle
Oxbow
Estevan
Wayburn
Radville
Milestone
Assiniboia
Gravelbourg
Ponteix
Shaunavon
Gull Lake
Herbert
Cabri
Leader
Maple Creek

Alberta, British Columbia, Yukon, Northwest Territories

Caravan 7

Alberta (Part 1)

Milk River
Raymond
Magrath
Cardston
Pincher Creek
Blairmore
Coleman
Fort MacLeod
Claresholm
Nanton
High River
Black Diamond
Okotoks
Vulcan
Taber
Bow Island
Brooks
Bassano
Strathmore
Cochrane
Banff
Carstairs
Didsbury
Olds
Innisfail
Sylvan Lake
Rocky Mountain
    House
Lacombe

Rimbey
Ponoka
Wetaskiwin
Leduc
Devon
Edson
Hinton
Evansburg
Drayton Valley
Mayerthorpe
Whitecourt
Valleyview
Grande-Prairie
Beaverlodge

British Columbia

Dawson Creek
Chetwynd
Fort St. John
Fort Nelson

Yukon

Watson Lake
Teslin
Whitehorse
Haines Junction
Mayo
Dawson City

Alberta (Part 2)

Rycroft
Fairview
Grimshaw
Peace River
High Level

Northwest Territories

Hay River
Fort Providence
Rae
Yellowknife
Fort Smith

Alberta (Part 3)

Fort Vermilion
Manning
McLennan
High Prairie
Slave Lake
Athabasca
Lac-la-Biche
Cold Lake
Grand-Centre
Bonnyville
St. Paul
Vilna
Smoky Lake
Red Water
Westlock
Barrhead
Morinville
Ft. Saskatchewan
Vegreville
Myrnan
Vermilion
Wainwright
Viking
Camrose
Hardisty
Provost
Coronation

Consort
Oyen
Hanna
Castor
Stettler
Three Hills
Drumheller

British Columbia

Caravan 8

Langley
New Westminster
Port Coquitlam
White Rock
Ladner
Richmond
Sidney
Salt Spring Island
Sooke
Colwood
Shawnigan Lake
Duncan
Lake Cowichan
Chemainus
Ladysmith
Parksville
Qualicum
Albernis
Campbell River
Courtenay
Powell River
(via Nanaimo Ferry)
Sechelt
Squamish
West Vancouver
North Vancouver

Burnaby	Kinnaird	Houston
Surrey	Greenwood	Blackburn
Abbotsford	Osoyoos	Hixon
Cultus Lake	Oliver	Wells
Harrison Hot Springs	Penticton	Lac-la-Hache
Mission	Okanagan Falls	Clinton
Haney	Summerland	Barriere
Hope	Westbank	Chase
Boston Bar	Rutland	Salmon Arm
Lytton	Vernon	(& area)
Cache Creek	Lumby	Enderby
Merritt	Armstrong	Sicamous
Princeton	North Kamloops	Revelstoke
Keremeos	Ashcroft	Golden
Grand Forks	100-Mile House	Edgewater
Rossland	Williams Lake	Invermere
Trail	Quesnel	Canal Flats
Fruitvale	Vanderhoof	Kimberly
Salmo	Fort St. James	Fort Steele
Creston	Burns Lake	Galloway
Crawford Bay	Smithers	Fernie
Nelson	Terrace	Sparwood
Kaslo	Kitimat	
Slocan	Hazelton	

APPENDIX H

Car One

Here the land is born. We are in the great rain forests before the last ice age. Then time etches its changes; as ice recedes we see signs of an early man. What was he like? We wonder. Across the Bering Strait come the first immigrants but our knowledge of them is scant and our first accurate view of a culture is that of the west coast Haida Indians and, later, the eastern Indians. All this we experience through the skills of designers, technicians, artists and craftsmen. They take us into Indian villages and they also transport our minds between past and present for comparisons of today with yesterday. We see the incense burner and the ornament from a pagoda, symbols which remind us that the Orient held the new riches wanted by the old European world — the incentive to discovery. But the European explorers, who found this other world in their path, discovered that it had its own riches in furs and gold, and the missionaries who followed saw a potential harvest in men's souls.

Car Two

Exploring new horizons called for rare skill and courage. We stand on the deck of a Viking ship and hear the sound of the wild sea — perhaps off Labrador's coast. We see a model of Cartier's ship, and a plank from the original hull. The electronic map traces the routes of Cabot, Cartier, Hudson and the many others. Canada's first great hero, Champlain, who attempted the first settlement of Nova Scotia, stands in life-size near his astrolabe and a 1632 Canada map of his own making. Here too, ancient engravings of his own sketches reveal Champlain the soldier as he sees himself, and Quebec City's first house built by this same man. We move through the exploration of yesterday and today, symbolized by the canoe and the bush aeroplane's pontoon. We live with early immigrants, horrified by disturbingly realistic steerage-class conditions on an early sailing ship, and share their hopes of leaving misery behind in Europe and of finding a better life in the new world.

Car Three
Entering the era of settlement we step into a French seignorial house. Through the drawing room window we look upon a scene typical of early nineteenth-century French Canada. No matter what our backgrounds, do we not feel that old France as well as old Britain contributed much to our heritage? Old and modern tools and machines (the means of settlement) and their economic and sociological implications contrast the efforts of the pioneers with life and work today. More exhibits illustrate the pre-Confederation state of confusion — the isolation of communities and colonies and the pressures from the United States. Now we move into the Confederation Chamber, 1867, and find emotional stability in the birth of an idea: Canadian Confederation. Here, for the first time, we find the Centennial symbol prominent — with four triangles coloured, representing the first four entrants into Confederation: Ontario, Quebec, New Brunswick and Nova Scotia.

Car Four
Travelling quickly through time we experience the growing pains of the period from 1867 to 1876. (Our visit to an old printing shop reminds us of Confederation's birth pains because it contains the printing press of Nova Scotia's Joseph Howe which he used to flail the Confederation idea, then to praise it). We meet the prime ministers of the period: Macdonald and Mackenzie. More provinces join: Manitoba 1870, British Columbia 1871 and Prince Edward Island 1873. Does the sight of Sitting Bull's rifle and the Sioux headdress stir sympathy deep within us? That great force, the North West Mounted, is born. We live through the Riel Rebellion. The Hudson's Bay Grant, of an area larger than some continents, creates a Canada that stretches to three oceans. We go on to complete the rail line to the Pacific, experience the wild excitement of the Klondike rush, meet Prime Ministers Thompson,

Abbot, Tupper, Bowell and Laurier. From now on, Canada negotiates her own treaties. We learn of greater wealth in gold, iron, copper and uranium.

Car Five

The pace of life quickens as the nineteenth century ends. Our troops start dying, for the first time for someone else, somewhere else — in the Boer War. 1900 to 1910 is the era of "the homesteaders" on the prairies. Alberta and Saskatchewan join in 1905. We see from horizon to horizon a widening of the mosaic by people from Eastern Europe. Amundsen, at last, forces the Northwest Passage. A recruiting streetcar invites us on a "Free Trip to Europe..." and a terrible war. Inside a dugout roofed by corrugated iron and sand bags we peer out on no-man's land amid the frightening din of trench warfare. The prime minister is Sir Robert Borden, followed by Arthur Meighen. The twenties roar in with flappers, peep shows and player pianos. The roar ends with a stock crash, heralding the sad, drab thirties. Intellectual ferment brings new political ideas. Prime Minister Bennett presides. Then, in 1939, front pages cry "Canada at War With Germany," "Warsaw Hurls Back Invaders." But Warsaw hadn't.

Car Six

Again the torch is seized by willing hands in 1939 — so soon after the terrible war of 1914-18. Now a production nation, Canada turns out warplanes, tanks and ships on the home front while her heroes fight and die abroad. We witness the bomber raids, the fighting on land and sea, and the great mushroom cloud — a huge question mark that forces our concern for the world's future. It is Prime Minister Mackenzie King who announces the war's end. Having adjusted to peace, Canadians make new achievements in science, politics, medicine, industry, the arts and international affairs. Newfoundland joins to complete the Centennial symbol. We meet the prime ministers of our time — St. Laurent, Diefenbaker and Pearson. Perhaps it is here one feels so brief an adventure through history is not enough. Perhaps one yearns to spend time to read and gain a deeper understanding of the past. We also see images of the future suggesting that a greater story is about to begin. Who will make that story? Who, but us, will create the future Canada?

APPENDIX I

CENTENNIAL COMMISSION TOTAL EXPENDITURES
1963 TO MARCH 31, 1968
expressed in 1992 dollars*

**Programs and projects
of national significance**
(Appendix J) $158,295,564

**Grants to provinces for approved
projects of a lasting nature:**
  Confederation Memorial Program
  (Appendix K) 87,812,420
  Centennial Grants Program
  (Appendix L) 59,109,985

  146,922,405 146,922,405

Administration:
  Salaries 19,228,259
  Exhibits, displays and films 12,615,565
  Professional and special services 9,433,771
  Travel 2,663,039
  Telephone and telegraph 1,347,553
  Accommodation 1,435,980
  Informational programs and publications 1,678,854
  Stationery, supplies and office equipment 1,588,911
  Employee benefits 1,092,592
  Accounting services 729,120
  National Conference on the
    Centennial of Confederation 731,783
  Other 1,693,196

  54,238,623

Grand Total of Expenditures **$359,456,592**

*The costs displayed in this appendix and in Appendices J, K and L are what it would take in current dollars to accomplish what was done in 1967 — more than quadruple the dollars spent by the Centennial Commission during its existence 1963-67. An inflation factor of 4.2 (420%) as provided by Statistics Canada was applied to the 1967 costs.

APPENDIX J

CENTENNIAL COMMISSION PROGRAMS AND PROJECTS OF NATIONAL SIGNIFICANCE
1963 TO MARCH 31, 1968

Confederation Train and Caravans	$47,903,784
Performing Arts	16,276,915
Promotion of Centennial Abroad	6,538,073
Youth Travel — Federal/Provincial	8,774,926
National Capital	2,316,724
Youth Travel — Voluntary Organizations	4,793,569
Promotion of Train and Caravans	3,797,703
Promotion of Performing Arts	2,412,245
Centennial Medals and Medallions	2,097,598
Publications Assistance	2,318,060
Canadian Folk Arts	1,831,998
Films	3,017,503
Centennial Athletics	3,643,601
Voyageur Canoe Pageant	1,489,400
Son et Lumière	1,923,171
Canadian Universities Participation	1,619,352
International Assistance	1,330,938
Visual Arts	1,108,254
Student Involvement	489,632
Promotion of Centennial Symbol	647,804
Isolated Communities	602,797
Participation by Indians	835,724
Promotion of *Voyageur* Canoe Pageant	551,368
Representation and Ceremonies	330,275
Community Exchanges	688,149
Special Provincial Projects	307,322
Community Improvement	615,766
The Dictionary of Canadian Biography	672,000
Les Jeunesses Musicales du Canada	735,000
Promotion of Youth Travel	221,067

(continued)

Spectacle on the Hill	273,979
Canada Guide	131,305
Special Travel — Spectacle on the Hill Participants	118,801
Church Participation	459,862
Tree and Shrub Planting	129,826
National Centennial Guide	1,344,000
Fathers of Confederation Memorial	
Citizens Foundation	11,760,000
Canadian Centenary Guide	1,454,242
Associations des Anciens — College de Montréal	210,000
Historical Re-enactments	604,220
National Arts Centre	18,784,970
P.E.I. Centenary Observance	420,000
Canadian Conference of the Arts	164,766
Canadian Museum Association	154,350
Promotion — Other	1,362,291
Other Projects Under $25,000	1,032,234

$158,295,564

APPENDIX K

CENTENNIAL COMMISSION GRANTS TO PROVINCES FOR APPROVED PROJECTS OF A LASTING NATURE: Confederation Memorial Program

Newfoundland
Arts and Cultural Centre — St. John's $10,500,000

Nova Scotia
Medical Science Building — Halifax   10,395,075

New Brunswick
Provincial Administrative Building — Fredericton   10,500,000

Quebec
Le Grand Théâtre de Quebec — Quebec City   5,803,325

Ontario
Centre of Science and Technology — Toronto   10,500,000

Manitoba
Concert Hall — Winnipeg   10,500,000

Saskatchewan
Performing Arts Centre — Regina   1,753,895
Performing Arts Centre — Saskatoon   5,250,000

Alberta
Museum and Archives Building — Edmonton   10,500,000

British Columbia
Museum and Archives Building — Victoria   10,313,134

Yukon
Museum and Civic Administration Building
— Whitehorse   1,050,000

Northwest Territories
Regional Library — Hay River   746,991

                                                    $87,812,420

Note: The Confederation Memorial Buildings at Charlottetown, Prince Edward Island, are included in Appendix J under the entry "Fathers of Confederation Memorial Citizens Foundation."

APPENDIX L

Centennial Commission Grants to Provinces for Approved Projects of a Lasting Nature: Centennial Grants Program

Newfoundland	87 projects	$1,093,075
Prince Edward Island	30 projects	331,821
Nova Scotia	36 projects	2,824,135
New Brunswick	56 projects	1,889,731
Quebec	56 projects	17,432,201
Ontario	551 projects	17,751,384
Manitoba	173 projects	3,638,372
Saskatchewan	399 projects	2,711,495
Alberta	275 projects	4,981,280
British Columbia	333 projects	6,251,771
Yukon Territory	11 projects	124,408
Northwest Territories	1 project	80,312
	2,008 projects	**$59,109,985**

Chapter Notes

Chapter 2 — *History*

P. 15: "The union...proved to be too restrictive...those of Canada West.": Swainson, Donald, *Ontario and Confederation, Centennial Historical Booklet Series,* Centennial Commission, Ottawa, 1967, p. 5.

P. 19: "...that no Prince Edward Island delegation would leave the island.": MacNutt, W.S., *The Maritimes and Confederation, Centennial Historical Booklet Series,* Centennial Commission, Ottawa, 1967, p. 4.

P. 24: "...not one of the French Canadians had been born in France.": Whitelaw, W.M., *The Quebec Conference, Canadian Historical Booklet Series,* Centennial Commission, Ottawa, 1967, p. 15.

P. 26: "The object of the act...independence and autonomy": Attributed to Lord Watson. Whitelaw, *Quebec Conference,* p. 20.

P. 27: "Governor James Douglas of Vancouver Island...extending his authority to the mainland.": Morton, W.L., *The West and Confederation, Centennial Historical Booklet Series,* Centennial Commission, Ottawa, 1967, p. 10.

Chapter 3 — *Canada in the Sixties*

P. 32: "It was a prosperous decade...which established free trade in automobiles and parts.": *The Canadian Encyclopedia*. Edmonton: Hurtig Publishers, 1988, p. 652.

P. 32: ..."the gross national product had exceeded $50 billion a year...": Edmonds, Alan, *The Years of Protest 1960-1970*. Ottawa: National Science Library of Canada, 1977.

P. 32: "In 1965 the average annual family income...twice as high as the national average.": Edmonds, *Years of Protest*.

P. 32: "During his tenure...gave western farmers a boost.": *The Canadian Encyclopedia*, p. 594.

P. 32: "The 'Northern Vision' that he preached...resulted in some economic development.": *The Canadian Encyclopedia*, p. 594.

P. 33: "Between 1941 and 1951...to more than 18 million.": Woodcock, George, *A Social History of Canada*. Toronto: Penguin Books Canada Ltd.,

P. 34: "By 1963, the university population was four times higher than in 1940...": *The Canadian Encyclopedia*, p. 2219.

P. 34: "They succeeded in having some effect...": *The Canadian Encyclopedia*, p. 2087.

P. 34: "And then there were the draft dodgers...": Edmonds, *Years of Protest*.

P. 34: "...which included elements of anarchism and heretical Marxism...": Woodcock, *Social History*, p. 379.

P. 34: "...and attached itself to the hippie culture..." Woodcock, *Social History*, p. 381.

P. 34: "...to impose controls that were unacceptable..." *The Canadian Encyclopedia*, p. 163.

P. 35: "...Paul Martin played an important part...": *The Canadian Encyclopedia*, p. 163.

P. 36: "...Canada did not demonstrate enough independence...": Robert Bothwell, and John Drummond. *English Canada Since 1945, Politics and Provincialism.* Toronto: University of Toronto Press, 1989, p. 262.

P. 36: "...to set up nationalist organization by the end of the decade.": *The Canadian Encyclopedia*, p. 1433.

P. 37: "He published classic works...works of Canadian fiction.": *The Canadian Encyclopedia*, p. 1256.

P. 38: "But when Quebec...to foreign countries — Ottawa.": *The Canadian Encyclopedia*, p. 1813.

P. 38: "The most significant...1966 Quebec election.": *The Canadian Encyclopedia*, p. 1980.

P. 39: "Incredibly...meant greater demands on the rest of Canada.": Bothwell, *English Canada Since 1945*, p. 251.

P. 40: "Inuit carvings...in the late fifties.": *The Canadian Encyclopedia*, p. 1087.

Bibliography

Abrahams, Roger et al., *"The Language of Festivals: Celebrating the Economy" in V. Turner (ed.)* Celebrations: Studies in Festivity and Ritual. *Washington: Smithsonian Institute Press, 1982.*

Allwood, John, The Great Exhibitions. *Toronto: Studio Vista, 1977.*

An Act Respecting the Observance of the Centennial of Confederation in Canada. *Assented to 29th September 1961, 9-10 Elizabeth II, Chapter 60.*

Bascam, William, *"The Myth-Ritual Theory,"* Journal of American Folklore, *1970, Vol. 70, pp. 103-114.*

Berton, Pierre, The Comfortable Pew. *Toronto: McClelland & Stewart, 1965.*

Cardinal, Harold, The Unjust Society. *Edmonton: Hurtig Publishers, 1969.*

Centennial Historical Booklet Series. *Ottawa: Centennial Commission, 1967:*
Bonenfant, J.C., The French Canadians and The Birth of Confederation
Cornell, D. G., The Great Coalition.
Farr, D.L.M., Great Britain and Confederation.
Hamelin, Jean, First Years of Confederation.

MacNutt, W.S., The Maritimes and Confederation.

Morton, W.L., The West and Confederation.

Roby, Yves, The United States and Confederation.

Swainson, D., Ontario and Confederation.

Waite, P.B., The Charlottetown Conference.

Whitelaw, W.M., The Quebec Conference.

Chase, Richard A., *"Fairs and Festivals,"* Man-Environment Systems, *1977 (May), Vol. 7(3), pp. 117-144.*

Cole, Mary S., *"Ritual and Therapy: Casting a Circle of Change,"* Pratt Institute of Creative Arts Therapy Review, *1990, Vol. 11, pp.13-21.*

Cohn, W.H., *"A National Celebration: The Fourth of July in American History"* in Cultures, *1976, Vol. 3 (2), pp. 141-156.*

Connerton, Paul, How Societies Remember. *Cambridge: Cambridge University Press, 1989.*

Farber, Carole et al., *"High, Healthy, and Happy: Ontario Mythology on Parade"* in F.E. Manning *(ed.)* The Celebration of Society: Perspectives on Contemporary Cultural Performance. *London, Ontario: Congress of Social and Humanistic Studies, 1983.*

Frazer, James, The Golden Bough. *London, England: Macmillan, 1978.*

Grant, George P., Lament for a Nation. *Ottawa: Carleton University Press, 1982.*

Handelman, Don, Models and Mirrors: Towards an Anthropology of Public Events. *Cambridge: Cambridge University Press, 1990.*

Harrison, Jane E., Ancient Art and Ritual. *New York: Greenwood Press, 1969.*

Hobsbawn, Eric, The Invention of Tradition. *Cambridge: Cambridge University Press, 1983.*

International Encyclopedia of the Social Sciences. *Chicago: Encyclopedia Britannica Inc., 1982.*

Isambert, F.A., *"Feasts and Celebrations: Some Critical Reflections on the Idea of Celebration,"* Humanitas. *Vol. 5, pp. 29-42.*

Iso-Ahola, Seppo E., *"Towards a Social Psychology of Recreational Travel,"* Leisure Studies, *1983 (Jan), Vol. 2(1), pp. 45-56.*

LaMarsh, Judy, Memoirs of a Bird in a Gilded Cage. *Toronto: Canadian National Institute for the Blind, 1983.*

Manning, F.E. *(ed.),* The Celebration of Society: Perspectives on Contemporary Cultural Performance. *London, Ontario: Congress of Social and Humanistic Studies, 1983.*

Moore, Sally & B. Myerhoff *(eds.),* Secular Ritual. *Amsterdam: Van Gorcum, 1977.*

Pickering, W.S.F., *"Persistence of Rites of Passage: Towards an Explanation,"* British Journal of Sociology, *Vol. 25, pp. 63-78.*

Turner, Victor *(ed.),* Celebrations: Studies in Festivity and Ritual. *Washington: Smithsonian Institute Press, 1982.*

Warner, W. Lloyd, American Life: Dream and Reality. *Chicago: University of Chicago Press, 1953.*

Warner, W. Lloyd, The Living and The Dead: A Study of the Symbolic Life of Americans. *New Haven: Yale University Press, 1959.*

CENTENNIAL-RELATED HOLDINGS IN THE NATIONAL ARCHIVES OF CANADA

Record Group 69: Centennial Commission
Manuscript Group 28: Canadian Centenary Council
Record Group 71:
Canadian Corporation for the World Exhibition

The total shelf space occupied by this original material is 146.6 metres (the length of a football field).

The staff at the National Archives are as helpful as one could possibly imagine, and quickly take the mystery out of how to access material.

Students, academics, researchers, planners and implementers of anniversaries in this and future generations can be assured of finding rich and rewarding veins as they prospect in the 146.6 metres of Centennial material on deposit.

Index